Heaven's Gateway to a Blissful Marriage for Him

Names

Date

A Prophetic Model for Men with Prayer Sets for
Marriage Preparation or Restoration

HEAVEN'S GATEWAY TO A
BLISSFUL MARRIAGE

For Him

Second Edition

Ebenezer Gabriels & Abigail Ebenezer-Gabriels

Explore the Blissful Marriage Community and Resources

at

www.blissfulmarriageuniversity.com

19644 Club House Road Suite 815
Gaithersburg, Maryland 20886
www.EbenezerGabriels.Org
hello@ebenezergabriels.org

Dedication

THE LORD GOD OF MARRIAGES

To God in His Holy Kingdom
To the Lord our God who sits upon His Holy Altar
To the Bridegroom, Jesus Son of God
To the Upcoming Supper of the Lamb
To the Author of Marriages

Contents

Preparing for the Marriage Journey

Think about marriage as a new car being assembled by engineers. Different components are coupled together by Engineers to make the automobile fit for travel. Now let's assume there were two cars being produced. There are two teams of Engineers working. The first team, Engineer A followed closely the prescribed process for the car assembly. The quality work produced excellent results.. Team B also builds automobiles, but pays little detail during car production and has no quality control process in place. The two teams eventually produce two sets of cars. Which car do you think is likely to survive the test of the road?

Many marriages fail not because the couples did not do it right, they did all the counseling, attended all the training, and everything seemed good. The revelation of God you have in marriage, and your obedience to walk in God's light will open up heaven's door of bliss for your marriage. You are called to approach marriage, first as a spiritual journey requiring you to yield to the Holy Spirit in all marital concerns. Marriage is also a mission, a mission of God's kingdom committed into your good hands by Jesus, to bring heaven's glory to the earth.

The exchange between Eve and the serpent at Eden shut down the major gateways where God's treasures are released into marriages. Similar exchanges persist today, though disguised in various ways, and are responsible for the fall of many marriages today. With the redemption powers in the blood of the Lamb, Heaven's Gateway to a Blissful Marriage shines the light of God's knowledge into the 10 major gateways that every man must subdue before heaven's atmosphere is opened and released, this atmosphere of worship translates into a blissful marriage, here on earth.

First written in 2018, In the 2nd edition of the book, Heaven's Gateway to a Blissful Marriage, Ebenezer & Abigail share revelations, guides, concepts, models and prayers to open the gateways and heaven's atmosphere upon your marriage to usher the bliss from God's presence into your marriage. This book - Heaven's Gateway to a Blissful Marriage for Him, is a guide for men whether single, or married to bring heaven's glory into their marriage.

How to Use Heaven's Gateway to a Blissful Marriage Readiness for Her Book Effectively

1. A book for the woman, single or married, for marriage preparation or restoration to walk you into the gateways of the principles of God's kingdom which leads to a blissful marriage

2. This book discusses and walks through the 10 Faulty Gateways of the first Marriage between Adam and Eve.

3. This book has 10 chapters, and addresses how each of the gateways to a blissful marriage was shut down by the enemy. Each of these chapters gateway, and offers also offers heaven's perspective into these 10 gateways and God's solution to them

4. This book shares title chapters with the men's version because the gateways are the same.

5. Some chapters in this book addresses marriage concepts mainly from the perspective of the woman

6. Other chapters addresses concepts from the perspective of both men and women - to teach women important concepts to be learned in their marital relationships with men

7. There are other chapters that teach both man and the woman the same concepts that are material to their marital relationship.

8. Come together with your spouse-to-be to discuss learns learned

9. Understand the concept, so you can apply the knowledge gained to complete exercises in the Heaven's Gateway to a Blissful Marriage Workbook For Her (Sold separately)

10. Grab a copy of your Bible and study your bible alongside as you read the book

11. Pray the prayers in each chapter.

Chapter 1

The Gateway of the Foundations

Marriages must scale through the gateway of the foundations. The first marriage was held in Eden; this was also the first instance when the marriage doors were opened to troubles. First, a major door was opened to the enemy when the enemy deceived Eve, and disobedience entered marriage. Disobedience as recorded in the Scripture carries the weight as the sin of witchcraft. This opened their marriage to hardships on multiple fronts. Similarly, many couples face similar hardships in marriage, even though Jesus has brought salvation and His blood has become the atonement for sins. For these reasons, couples need to learn about the early blunders in the first marriage and barring their upcoming or current marriage before the Lord, so the hand of the Lord brings healing to these critical areas, and access to God's bliss can be released.

The 10 Faulty Gateways of the First Marriage: Lesson for You as a Husband from Adam's Failure

The diagram below is red clockwise, starting from worship altars and ending at the need for Deliverance

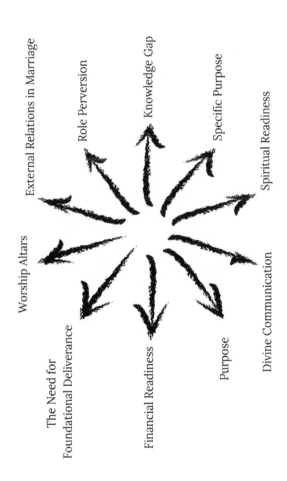

The Fall of the First Marriage

Worship Altars: Adam and Eve worshiped God in the garden through their service. We define worship as any act that delights God. Serving God at Eden was also worship.

- Every marriage is ordained as a worship altar to the Lord. The husband is the minister of God upon that altar, who ministers alongside with his wife and to his family.
- Marriage is holy to the Lord.

External Relations: Any third party that does not bring life or support the agenda of God in a marriage is a serpent. Serpent, the external party came to infiltrate and deceive Eve out of God's instruction which also translates to worship. External relations, if not handled well, can ruin the testimony of men in their marriages. The absence of Adam in the conversation between Eve and the serpent might have exposed Eve to the serpent's deception.

- The husband must pray for his wife against the spirit of deception.
- The husband must actively engage the wife, helping her husband that important family decisions cannot be made alone.

Role Perversion: Eve, was deceived to take the role of her husband in deciding to partake in the fruit of the forbidden tree. Genesis 3:1 *'Now the serpent was more cunning than any beast of the field which the Lord God had made. And he said to the woman, "Has God indeed said, 'You shall not eat of every tree of the garden'?"* Genesis 3:1 shares how roles were perverted *"Now the serpent was more cunning than any beast of the field which the Lord God had made. And he said to the woman, "Has God indeed said, 'You shall not eat of every tree of the garden'?"* Since this is an important family ordinance, the husband was left out of the conversation to deceive Eve, placing Eve in the wrong place and ensnaring her to step in to make a decision she was not responsible for.

- The husband is the head of the household, and the couple must understand their roles. Important decisions cannot be made where the head of the household is not present or aware.
- The husband must continue to pray for the protection of his role as the head of the family.

Knowledge Gap: Satan deceived Eve into thinking there were knowledge gaps in their lives, and that the solution was to close that knowledge gap (knowledge gap is explained in an entire chapter. Genesis 3:4-5 reveals the knowledge gap presented to Eve *"Then the serpent* *said to the woman, "You will not surely die. For God knows that on the day you eat of it your eyes will be opened, and you will be like God, knowing good and evil.*

- The husband should continually remind his wife that all profitable and beneficial knowledge comes from the Lord.
- In prayers, husbands should respond by praying that himself, his wife will not be susceptible to satanic wisdom

Specific Purpose: The specific purpose of Adam, which is to tend the garden was lost here when he was cast out of the land of his purpose, and he could no longer do what God created him to do originally.

- Every husband has a unique purpose, which must be identified before marriage.
- Where purpose is not identified, the husband stands a chance of his wife helping him find his purpose. As a rule of thumb, no one can help others find their purpose, since purpose is embedded in the soul. We discussed this in detail in our book, "Unprofaned Purpose".

Spiritual Readiness: Adam had an acute spiritual understanding which was reflected when he named all the animals. This was because he was pure and complete as God had created Him as a copy of Himself.

He became vulnerable to his deceived wife when he was not spiritually alert or ready to respond when he obeyed his wife and partook in the forbidden fruit, resulting in becoming exposed to earthly wisdom, and a new understanding of nakedness. He went from a place of spiritual alertness to a place of spiritual defilement. The demonic knowledge that was introduced brought profanity.

- The husband is the head of the household, and the couple must understand their roles. Important decisions cannot be made where the head of the household is not present or aware.
- The husband must continue to pray for the protection of his role as the head of the family.

The Loss of Divine Communication: Their spiritual state changed from being spiritually secured to spiritual exposed. They went from a place where they were benefiting from God's voice to being cast out of God's presence. Usually, the couple had access to God's presence as seen in Genesis 3:8 *"And they heard the sound of the Lord God walking in the garden in the cool of the day, and Adam and his wife hid themselves from the presence of the Lord God among the trees of the garden"*. This privilege was lost when they were cast out of Eden, and the voice of God became scarce.

- To succeed as God's representative in the family, the husband must desire to hear from God, and develop a strong spiritual life to know the mind of the Father and hear from Him.

The Loss of Marital Purpose: Their purpose to work together as companions in Eden was lost. *"Then the eyes of both of them were opened, and they knew that they were naked; and they sewed fig leaves together and made themselves coverings"* - Genesis 3:7

- The husband has a primary goal to defend their marital purpose. The wife has the responsibility of supporting and defending the purpose. We will examine what the marital purposes look like.

Financial Loss: The couple's economic life became open to uncertainties and hardship as they were cast out into the world. Financial loss was one of the consequences of disobedience as seen in Genesis 3:17 *"Then to Adam He said, "Because you have heeded the voice of your wife, and have eaten from the tree of which I commanded you, saying, 'You shall not eat of it':"Cursed is the ground for your sake;In toil you shall eat of it All the days of your life".*

- One of the husband's primary assignments is to provide for finances for the family, while the woman helps him deliver an assignment.

- When this curse is not fully broken, couples suffer financial hardships at the beginning of their marriage.
- Where this curse is at work in a man's life, it manifests as poverty and the wives become the financiers of their family.

The Need for Deliverance: The consequences of disobedience opened the couple up to curses, and many of the treasures which were previously accessible to them were closed. *The Scripture notes; "And as for Seth, to him also a son was born; and he named him Enosh. Then men began to call on the name of the LORD"* - *Genesis* 4:6 The husband is called to a purpose of God, and the wife is called to help him, but since they disobeyed; hardship gets in the way. As a result, they faced many consequences and curses, and this was the first time that humans began to pray to the Lord.

First, a major door was opened to the enemy when the enemy deceived Eve, and disobedience entered the marriage. Disobedience as recorded in the Scriptures carry the same weight as the sin of witchcraft. This exposed their marriage to hardships on multiple fronts even though Jesus has brought salvation and His blood has become the atonement for sins. For these reasons, couples need to learn about the early blunders in the first marriage, and bearing their upcoming or current marriage before the Lord, so the hand of the Lord brings healing to these critical areas, and access to God's bliss can be released.

What's in your Foundation?

Foundations are the base for the building blocks of marriage. The foundation of marriages exists long before you meet your spouse. Psalm 11:3 - *"If the foundations are destroyed, what can the righteous do"*? The study of foundations is paramount to the success of any marriage. Where there is darkness in the foundation, and people go into marriage, they encounter all types and sizes of trouble in marriage. This explains why God has informed us to prayerfully educate you on this, and to shine His light into your foundation, so that His light will chase out all darkness in your foundation, and your marriage can be centered around the light of Jesus Christ.

The foundation of marriage is the structure on which your marriage will or stands upon. The foundation forms the underlying ground for marriages to thrive on. Foundations begin long before you start thinking about marriage. Your foundation could be your childhood, or long before you got here. Any part of your past that affects or could impact your marriage is the foundation of your marriage.

The fall which began with Adam and Eve has brought more complex problems into couples' foundations, which must be addressed and resolved before their marriage can encounter the bliss of the Lord Jesus.

EXAMPLES OF FOUNDATIONS PEOPLE BRING INTO THEIR MARRIAGES

A Look into Tony's Foundation: General Patterns

Tony is 30. He's good looking, graduated the best of his class; and found a girl he likes to marry. Tony is the last of 5 children. Tony's older sibling had recorded a sudden turn of events the moment they got engaged to their future spouse; they lost their jobs, and finances became shaky as they got closer to wedding dates; Some of them had called off their weddings because of similar reasons. Tony thought this was a coincidence; he summoned some courage to propose; He proposed to his sweetheart and had a beautiful weekend thinking of his new reality and title, "husband-to-be". When he got to work on Tuesday; his badge denied him access into the building, the security came to inform him to follow up with HR as his contract had ended on Monday. Tony's family pattern of job loss at the point of marriage is part of his foundation. This is an occurrence in his family line that affects marriage

Understanding Your Foundation

Foundations extend beyond the personal history of these individuals. The foundation goes beyond what we see with our eyes. It is made up of the spiritual atmospheres of the background that we passed through; what even makes it more complicated is that parents come from different backgrounds; then our background is interwoven with at least two other backgrounds; which makes the subject of foundations quite complex. Tony is unlikely to identify the causes of the patterns in his family.

Blended Families

There are different types of foundations people bring into marriages, and this can lead to the need to understand what God has in plan for couples who have kids prior to marriage and looking to build a blended family.

There are different types of foundations people bring into marriages, and this can lead to the need to understand what God has in plan for couples who have kids prior to marriage and looking to build a blended family.

There are two main keys to be known about blended families

- Blended families were not part of God's plan for marriages.
- God has a solution for blended families, and this solution usually requires hard work.

Couples who know that their marriage would require a blended family must get the education on blended family, prior to proceeding into a marriage.

MANIFESTATIONS OF EVIL IN FOUNDATIONS: THE SEVEN DEADLY TOXINS IN THE FOUNDATION OF MARRIAGES

There are 7 major toxins which are indicators of major problems in marriage foundations. These toxins, if allowed to remain as couples head into a marriage, will bring affliction into that marriage. When approaching marriage, the husband-to-be- must be willing to work with his bride-to-be together to address any existence of these toxins without shame, bias, judgment or condemnation in both their lives to receive the freedom of passage that comes from the blood of Jesus for their marriage. These toxins usually become heavy spiritual baggage, and when brought into the marriage, weighs sink the destiny of a marriage.

When these items are discussed and brought to the Lord in prayers, the Lord responds to the prayer of unity between two individuals looking to become one. The following are the most ways that foundational problems manifest. They are also the most potent foundational problems to bring into marriage without addressing.

Foundation of Sexual Activities; Sexual relations is only to occur within the boundaries of marriage. Sex is covenant in nature. Whenever married couples have sexual relations, they renew an ongoing vow. It is also an expression of worship to God in holy matrimony. Where sexual relations occur outside of marriage, there are strange and ungodly covenants formed. Where there have been sexual molestations, there is pollution in the foundation of the marriage and must be resolved.

Foundation of Abortion: Where abortion has occurred in the past, there is a demand for vengeance and the voice of the blood. Past abortion must be brought before God in repentance and must be discussed with your spouse to be.

Foundation of Incest: Incest occurs when you have had sexual relations with someone from your kin, *"None of you shall approach anyone who is near of kin to him, to uncover his nakedness: I am the Lord"* - Leviticus 18:6. Where there has been incest in your family; sexual relations between siblings, or between blood relatives, there is a foundation of incest somewhere in your background and you need to deal with it with the power of prayers.

Foundation of Idolatry: Prior to getting married, you should check your background for prior worship of other gods. Leviticus 19:4 notes *'Do not turn to idols, nor make for yourselves molded gods: I am the Lord your God.* Where there has been the worship of other gods, it must be checked whether salvation has occurred and the parties have come to Jesus as Lord and Savior. Also, you need to check the foundation of your spouse-to-be for any false worship.

Foundation of Poverty: Poverty is one of the leading killers of marriage. Poverty is anti-marriage and disrupts the flow of finances in marriage. Poverty kills the flow of funds in marriage. Poverty prohibits the availability of resources in marriages. Poverty works in a process,

Where the process of poverty is not halted, it ruins God's agenda in marriages.

Foundations of Infirmity: Where individuals are prone to sickness, or spent a significant moment in their life in hospitalization, or where there is a family trait of infirmity, there is a foundation of infirmity that must be addressed.

Foundations of Witchcraft: Many people practice witchcraft, male and female, and never really move on from it. They learned to cast spells, or have graduated into rituals, steal virtues, plan sicknesses into lives, draw blood. This foundation of witchcraft must be addressed, and those involved must be completely delivered before they get into marriage. If witchcraft is in the foundation, for example, if the bride's mother is a witchcraft practitioner, her daughter's marriage is a potential target of destruction because witchcraft is the enemy of every good thing.

- Witchcraft will require the virtues from the marriage.
- Witchcraft may require the virtues from the upcoming children in that new marriage.
- Witchcraft may seek to pollute the marital bed. Many husbands   have been bewitched into

sleeping with their wife's mother or wife's sister or wife's friend.

As a man, you need to be charged up by the fire of the Holy Spirit, and be ready to snatch your wife-to-be out if there's witchcraft in the family-line, or if she is prone to witchcraft, so it does not ruin your purpose. Also, there may be witchcraft in your foundation, could be someone close to you in your bloodline operating in witchcraft, or you have been used to consulting witchcraft practitioners. You need to be delivered of this too, before proceeding into marriage.

Foundations of Polygamy: One of the spirits ravaging marriages is the spirit of polygamy. If parents or grandparents had multiple wives, multiple children by multiple mothers, children need to rise to break the hold of the spirit of polygamy before getting into marriage. Instances of spiritual polygamy today includes;

- When a spouse continues to see their ex after marriage.
- When a spouse continues in an adulterous relationship.

- Where your parents were promiscuous or cheated on each other, there is a foundation of polygamy
- Where your parents married more than one wife
- If you parents were involved in divorce, or you have been divorced before, there is a foundation of polygamy.
- If there there has been different births by different parents (your mother had children for multiple fathers, or your father had different children by multiple mothers, or you have had other children before planning on a new marriage) there is the foundation of polygamy.

Deliverance from the Foundational Strongholds

Foundational deliverance affords us the opportunity to send the power of God into our foundation and the blood of Jesus to cleanse us from all forms of unrighteousness.

> "If we say that we have no sin, we deceive ourselves, and the truth is not in us. If we confess our sins, He is faithful and just to forgive us our sins and to cleanse us from all unrighteousness. If we say that we have not sinned, we make Him a liar, and His word is not in us". 1 John 1:8-9 NKJV

- Foundational deliverance is attained by couples when they have fully committed their lives to the Lord Jesus.
- Foundational deliverance is possible where the couple or couples-to-be commits to be open to each other, in truth, without reservation.
- Foundational deliverance occurs where both couples are willing to close the doors to condemnation, shame, judgment or biases.

This is why we always recommend a foundational deliverance for every intending couple, that the Lord will go into their foundation, to uproot all evil, annd plan their marital lives on the immovable Rock .

Prayer Sets for the Man's Foundation

1. Lord Jesus, deliver me from all appearances of polygamy.
2. Lord Jesus, as I embark on this endeavor, let your light shine into the darkest part of my foundation, in the name of Jesus.
3. Let there be deliverance in my foundation in the name of Jesus.
4. Let the power of the Holy Ghost shine the light of God into every dark area of my foundation in the name of Jesus.
5. Lord Jesus, let there be light in the foundation of my marriage in the name of Jesus.
6. God, let there be no darkness in my marriage in the name of Jesus.
7. My temple is sanctified by the blood of Jesus. My body is not the habitation of demons, my body is sanctified by the precious blood of Jesus.
8. The spirit and grasp of death in my marriage is broken by the blood of Jesus.
9. The hold of the power of incest is broken over my life by the blood of Jesus.

10. The cry of the voice of incest is broken over my life in the name of Jesus.

11. The hold of the power of poverty is broken over my future marriage in the name of Jesus.

12. The hold of the spirit of infirmity is broken over my marriage by the blood of Jesus.

13. Lord Jesus, deliver my marriage from the toxins of darkness, in the name of Jesus

14. Let the blood off Jesus wipe past sexual sins in the name of Jesus.

15. Let the blood of Jesus wipe away the guilt of abortion and the voices seeking revenge against my life in the name of Jesus.

16. Father Lord, let the power in the blood of Jesus cancel every curse in my background hanging upon my neck as a result of incest in my foundations in the name of Jesus.

17. Lord Jesus, deliver me from the witchcraft powers in my foundation, in the name of Jesus.

18. Lord Jesus, deliver me from the influences of witchcraft powers in my foundation, in the name of Jesus.

19. Lord Jesus, deliver me from the influences of stargazers, mediums, soothsayers and false prophets in the name of Jesus.

20. Lord Jesus, visit my foundation and the foundation of my parents, and uproot all forms of polygamy in the foundation.

21. Lord Jesus, deliver me from the foundations of poverty, in the name of Jesus.

22. Lord Jesus, deliver me from the foundations of impulsive spending in the name of Jesus.

23. Lord Jesus, deliver me from the mindset of financial illiteracy, in the name of Jesus

24. Lord, uphold the mindset of consumerism that seeks to spend and not grow financially in the name of Jesus.

25. Lord Jesus, let the spirit of poverty be cast out of my life in the name of Jesus.

26. Lord Jesus, expose every enemy hiding in the blood to afflict my marriage, in the name of jesus.

27. Lord Jesus, expel every enemy hiding in the blood afflicting my marital life, in the name of Jesus.

28. Lord Jesus, deliver me from the foundation of infirmity.

29. Lord Jesus, deliver me from the infirmities that plagued the men in my family line, in the name of Jesus.

30. Lord Jesus, flow through my blood, and let your blood purge out every infirmity in my bloodline, in the name of Jesus.

31. Lord Jesus, visit my reproductive health as a man of your blood in the name of Jesus.

32. Lord, visit my womb with your blood for cleansing and purification in the name of Jesus.

33. Lord Jesus, visit my vital organs with your blood for cleansing and purification in the name of Jesus.

34. Fire of the Holy Spirit, purify my body, my male organs and all other vital parts of my body as a woman and I decree that there shall be no form of cancer recorded in my life in the name of Jesus.

35. Blood of Jesus, deliver my bloodline and marriage generational infirmity in the name of Jesus.

36. Lord Jesus, visit my marriage, and make all things new, in the name of Jesus.

Journal

Chapter 2

Divine Communications in Marriage

Divine communication is defined as the communication between the Lord and God's children, powered through spiritual giftings placed in us, through the Holy Spirit. Hearing from God is needed, especially where marriage plans are ahead. You will need to hear from God accurately to make the right decisions, and to live successfully in marriage.

SCRIPTURE
Hebrews 1:1-3 *God, who at various times and in various ways spoke in time past to the fathers by the prophets, has in these last days spoken to us by His Son, whom He has appointed heir of all things, through whom also He made the worlds;*

God still speaks and this opportunity must be leveraged to obtain the right information, at the right time through the right channel from the Lord.

It is God's desire to speak to you as a husband. You are a leader, and God has a lot of things to say to you. He will show you long-term plans, and how you need to work with your wife as a family to get to that destination. Abraham was a living example:

> "For I have known him, in order that he may command his children and his household after him, that they keep the way of the LORD, to do righteousness and justice, that the LORD may bring to Abraham what He has spoken to him." -
> **Genesis 18:19 NKJV**

Jacob's Marriage

When any man is set to get married, the enemy lays a snare for the man to be deceived to marry the wrong person.

> **Genesis 29:21-25 NKJV**
> *Then Jacob said to Laban, "Give me my wife, for my days are fulfilled, that I may go in to her." Laban gathered together all the men of the place and made a feast. Now it came to pass in the evening, that he took Leah his daughter and brought her to Jacob; and he went in to her. Laban gave his maid Zilpah to his daughter Leah as a maid. So it came to pass in the morning, that*

behold, it was Leah. And he said to Laban, "What is this you have done to me? Was it not for Rachel that I served you? Why then have you deceived me?"

In moments of prayer ministry, many men have ended up with the wrong women because of deception. Some of these men ask, "since I was deceived into marriage, can I divorce her"? The God we serve never changes, he honors covenants, once signed. This is seen in the book of Joshua 9 where the Gibeonites deceived Joshua, the leader of Israel into signing a treaty with them. Joshua could not separate Israel from the treaty when he realized they had been lied to. As a result, it is of utmost importance to hear from God before making a choice of wife.

You need divine communication for marriage because;

1. You need to marry the God-ordained spouse
2. You need to marry the spouse of purpose
    a. One whom have found the purpose of God
    b. One whom you have been assigned to help nurture and advance the purpose of God
    c. One that will lead your household in the ways of God's kingdom

The Right Information, the Right Time and the Right Channel

Every man needs to pray for the power of God that releases the needed information at the right time, through the right channel. You need this power to understand when it's time the Lord is bringing you in contact with the wife of your destiny, who she is, and how God will unveil this information to you.

A major insight God has spoken and confirmed to us in ministry is that people will usually have the opportunity to meet their God-ordained spouse at least once in a lifetime, maybe twice, and if they are highly favored for a season. Many people, especially women have mocked, joked with and trashed their God-ordained husbands, and have sought after men who were detrimental to their destiny. Some of the other common snares women find themselves in due to false revelations, and the inability to discern the voice of the Lord are:

1. The snare of falling into the marriage with the woman who has not come to the Lord.
2. The snare of falling into marriage with the woman man that was not ordained for you.
3. The snare of falling into marriage with the woman who will not offer any help.

4. The snare of getting into marriage with a woman who expects you to take over the leadership of the family.

The Day of Unveiling: The Manifestations on the Day You'll Find Your Wife

There's the day called the day of unveiling - it's the day when the Lord opens your eyes to find your wife, and the veil is taken off her face. It is truly the day of appointment with favor and prosperity, assuming you find your ordained wife. We explore the day of unveiling from Rebekka's story.

Genesis 24:11-21 NKJV

And he made his camels kneel down outside the city by a well of water at evening time, the time when women go out to draw water. Then he said, "O Lord God of my master Abraham, please give me success this day, and show kindness to my master Abraham. Behold, here I stand by the well of water, and the daughters of the men of the city are coming out to draw water. Now let it be that the young woman to whom I say, 'Please let down your pitcher that I may drink,' and she says, 'Drink, and I will also give your camels a drink'—let her be the one You have appointed for

Your servant Isaac. And by this I will know that You have shown kindness to my master." And it happened, before he had finished speaking, that behold, Rebekah, who was born to Bethuel, son of Milcah, the wife of Nahor, Abraham's brother, came out with her pitcher on her shoulder. Now the young woman was very beautiful to behold, a virgin; no man had known her. And she went down to the well, filled her pitcher, and came up. And the servant ran to meet her and said, "Please let me drink a little water from your pitcher."So she said, "Drink, my lord." Then she quickly let her pitcher down to her hand, and gave him a drink. And when she had finished giving him a drink, she said, "I will draw water for your camels also, until they have finished drinking." Then she quickly emptied her pitcher into the trough, ran back to the well to draw water, and drew for all his camels. And the man, wondering at her, remained silent so as to know whether the Lord had made his journey prosperous or not.

On the day of unveiling, many moving parts work together for God's glory when the mercy of God locates a man and he finds his wife. From the Scriptures above, there are different manifestations which may turn out to become testimonies or ruin the testimonies of men in search of a wife.

1. This was a time when women usually came out to draw water.
2. There is the possibility of the spirit of confusion taking over the reasoning of Abraham's servant who was out to search out a wife for Isaac.
3. There is the possibility of another woman being chosen over *Rebekah.*
4. There is the possibility of Rebekka not showing up according to the regular schedule
5. There is the possibility of Rebekka being at her worst behavior on the day the servant was in search of Isaac's bride.

Understanding the Reverse-Rebekkah Spirit: An Opposing Spirit to Finding the Wife of Your Destiny
These manifestations are seen regularly everywhere. Journeying in the prophetic has confirmed these biblical revelations severally. People who have closely encountered our prophetic ministry are aware that we will not release a Word to tell people, "this is the individual God wants you to marry". The reason is that God had brought us through a training on this subject early in our prophetic ministry journey. God may reveal that two people are a right fit for marriage, and other

parts of their foundations may not be revealed. These unrevealed parts may be areas that they are not willing to work on or improve on, so it becomes problematic and blames are pointed to anyone who shares a revelation of them being a right fit.

Also, many times, God has given the privilege of witnessing two individuals He has ordained to become husband and wife. Where this occurs, satan has a way of derailing to ensure that they never grow their relationship into marriage or lead them into all foolishness at the point of discovering each other. We have encountered a lot of the manifestations of what we call the **Reverse-Rebekkah spirits.**

Reverse-Rebekkah spirits are spirits contending against the revelation of Rebekkah as the wife of Isaac. Reverse-Rebekkah spirits presents Rebekkah's false identity, to exclude Rebekkah from being chosen as the right wife for Isaac. This spirit seeks to bring out the worst in Rebekkah.

1. Women picking up anger, malice, fights, the moments their husband-to-be gets into close proximity with them.
2. This spirit is responsible for women aligning with the wrong friends.
3. This spirit may invoke pride in women, especially when they begin to show off or exhibit arrogant pride. They may even play hard to get

4. This spirit may even ridicule the husband-to-be, or project a rude image of the woman, such that the potential groom forms the wrong impression of her and becomes irritated.

5. This spirit leads women to consult their friends or seek irrelevant approval before they connect with a potential spouse.

6. This spirit lures some of its victims to become missing in action on the day the spouse of their destiny will come searching for them. Something will usually disrupt their regular flow. They may stop going to work, to church, to a place where they are appointed to meet the husband of their destiny for no reason. This is often seen when a potential groom no longer sees a potential bride around, and begins to look for her, or ways to obtain her contact.

7. This spirit lures vulnerable captives to date the wrong man when the right man watches on and gets no opportunity or gets the wrong impression. Some men sought to ask a lady out, and before they see what's happening, someone else is already with her. This spirit seeks to match women with the wrong individuals, so they can lose the opportunity of being with the right individuals.

8. This spirit lures captives into a circle where all the men get an opportunity for sexual encounter in different relationships with same woman, ruining her testimony, such that her real husband has no desire whatsoever to be with that kind of woman.

9. This spirit gets its captives to play hard to get, and the husband of their destinies.

The Lord minister to an individual during a prophetic worship session. This individual had missed out on the spouse of her destiny, and the Lord described the calling of the husband she was supposed to be married to. She testified that she met this individual 30 years ago. The enemy's major goal is to prevent the right man from marrying the right woman. This is the utmost reason why divine communication is needed for marriages.

More Reasons You Need to Hear from God as a Husband

Hearing God When Choosing a Wife: First, you need to hear from God directly regarding whether the woman you are going to marry is your God ordained wife. Many husbands live to regret their marriage because they never heard from God before marrying their wives. A man once said, "I was dating her and she kept pestering me for marriage, and I said that's it, let's go get married, and this is how we ended up living miserably together". Another one said, "someone had a dream and told me that this is my wife". As a man whom the Lord has ordained for his purpose, you need to be sure beyond any doubt that you hear God show you your wife. We live in times where the devil is out to get men stuck in the wrong marriage with a wife that was not part of God's plan for them. There is a huge price to pay for making the wrong choice of wife.

- *Making the wrong choice of wife closes the door to purpose.*
- *Making the wrong choice of wife locks men out of God's purpose for them.*
- *Making the wrong choice of wife leads to a marital life of affliction and pains.*
- *Making the wrong choice of wife will lead you into a life of frustration.*
- *Making the wrong choice of wife could crash your spiritual life and set you against the Lord.*
- It is very expensive to marry the wrong woman, and it could cost you your soul.

Marrying the right woman is a blessing to many generations. If you marry the right woman, your marriage will be blessed, and generations after you will be blessed.

- *You will get all the help needed to fulfill your purpose when you marry the right woman.*
- *You will earn God's favor when you marry the right woman.*
- *God's leadership will reign in your household when you marry the right woman.*

The only prerequisite you need to marry the right woman is to hear from God and obey Him

Hearing God on How to Become the Best Husband: You need God to speak to you about how to become the best husband after Jesus' heart.

- *Husbands must be like Jesus, as He loved the church. Communication from God is needed to learn how to be like Jesus every time.*

Hearing God and Making Decisions: Decision making as a husband will require a deep walk in the spirit of God's wisdom. This is only possible when you hear from God. You need to hear from God to learn how to make God-approved decisions.

- You will need to hear from God to determine whether decisions you are about to make are from Him.

Hearing God and Learning to Love God's Way

You need to hear from God on how to love your wife. Loving your wife as Jesus does love the church will only be taught by the Lord.

- Women have needs that only the Lord knows and fully understands. When you hear from God, you will be sensitized to the needs of your wife, and God shows you the way she needs to be loved.
- If you do not love her right, the devil will present falsehood to deceive her, and open your marriage to battles.

Hearing God and Succeeding as a Husband

You need to hear from God to learn how to succeed in your calling as a husband. There are many moving parts to being the husband of God's calling, one of the ways to succeed in this call is to be in close communication with God. If you do not hear from God, your wife may seek directions from other sources outside of God, and this brings failure to your calling.

Hearing God as His Representative

You need to hear from God because you are representing God in your family. You cannot represent God effectively if you are not hearing Him speak.

How God Speaks to Husbands

In this section, we learn from Numbers 12:6 to learn some of the ways God speaks. Numbers 12:6 writes - Then He said, "Hear now My words: If there is a prophet among you, I, the LORD, make Myself known to him in a vision; I speak to him in a dream.

God speaks through visions, and He speaks through dreams. He also speaks through other ways. Students of the Marriage Readiness class are encouraged to learn how God speaks to them because this holds many advantages when getting married. We do not want you to hear God for the first time because it pertains to your marriage decision. We want you to hear from God all the time and adapt His voice into your everyday life as there is security in this.

God's Voice and Communication

God's voice gives the clarity and direction needed for all life's endeavors. The Scripture shares a major secret in Psalm 29 verse 4 "The voice of the Lord is powerful; The voice of the Lord is full of majesty". God's voice is indeed powerful. Those who get the opportunity to hear God's voice benefit from the power in there. Hearing God's voice before getting into marriage will turn that marriage into a powerful encounter. Intending couples will benefit from hearing God's voice in the following areas:

- The choice of your partner for marriage.
- The right time for you to enter into marriage.
- The type of wedding to have.
- The purpose of your marriage.

Divine Communications for Marriage

When it comes to marriage, God wants to be a part of your marriage decision. He wants to tell you when to marry, who to marry, the purpose of your marriage, what type of wedding to have and every other detail you can think about. God also wants you to have the choice to do what you wish, so He does not force communication. When you allow Him to speak to you, He will communicate the right steps to take. God speaks in many ways. As you learn how God speaks to you, you may figure out that He speaks to you through more than one channel. Hearing God takes a lot of practice. You will need to learn how He speaks to you, and test that he has spoken to you and that you heard right and translated correctly.

Four Steps of Validating Divine Information

Here are steps and the process of validating divine information, received before making marriage decisions. This can be applied to other decision making. We teach our students all the time. You can use the following test in hearing from God about your spouse-to-be and upcoming marriage.

Step 1: Ascertaining you heard from God. In this stage, you know for sure, God spoke to you. The voice you heard is of the Lord.

Step 2: **Processing Information Right:** The information I received from the Lord has been processed correctly, nothing is missing, nothing lost.

Step 3: **Interpreting Right:** I have interpreted what I heard correctly

Step 4: **Testing**: I am testing the information given to be sure it came from God; I process right and translate the details right. If I did everything from step 1 to step 3 correctly, I should have the right result from the Lord.

Type of Voices

There are different voices that could rise when making marriage decisions. The most trusted God is the voice of God, and it is desired that the voice of God becomes your primary source of divine communication

1. **The Voice of God:** God's voice is our desire for you to hear when it comes to making marriage decisions. God's voice will point you to the right person, will order your step and will not land you into a ditch. That's not all the case most times. Sometimes other voices speak, and here are some of the other types of voices that can speak forth during marriage decisions. God's voice is the primary way and ideal way to hear and center your marriage decision. You may hear other voices as a confirmation.

2. **The Word of God:** The voice of God is all over the word of God. If you cannot hear God's voice, the Word of God gives an opening into God's Word, hence you can still find His voice in His Word.

3. **The Voice of Self/Flesh;** The voice of the flesh is usually against the voice of God. The flesh is quick to always speak up especially when it wants to have its way. Sometimes the flesh speaks up and whispers into your ears saying this is him or this is her when God does not say so.

4. **The Voice of Parents:** Parents do want their children's best and may even hear from God concerning you. God sometimes speaks through the voices of authorities around us, but, when awaiting God's voice on marriage, respect and honor the voice of your parents, but much more importantly, hear God's voice for yourself before making this life-changing decision.

5. **The Voice of Spouse-to-be:** If your spouse-to-be hears God's voice for you both to go ahead, you must go and verify with the Lord. The voice of the spouse-to-be must be watched. She begins to pester you, nag at you, complain that her friends are getting married, or her parents are getting worried you're not proposing. She may even suggest she will take care of all the wedding expenses.

6. **The Voice of Friends:** The voices of friends and others may also rise, or God could be speaking through them, always going back to verify with the Lord. Also, the enemy can use the voice of friends in this way; their voices mock you for choosing her, or for not choosing her.

7. **The Voice of Logic:** God may use the voice of logic to approve your marriage choices, or simply to disapprove. The enemy also sometimes uses the voice of logic. When the enemy does this, the

man could make marriage decisions based on calculations. The voice of logic says, "she is making $40,000 now, in the next two years se should be making $80,000, this makes her a good candidate for marriage".

8. **The Voice of the Enemy**: Satan seeks to plant confusion, doubt, and lies when people are about to get married. Satan's voice is prominent when people have not learned how God speaks to them, or have not developed their spiritual gifts. The voice of the enemy says, "you cannot live without her, because the sex is good. The voice of the enemy also says, "if you do not marry her, no one else will marry you".

9. **The Voice of Bias:** The voice of bias is related to the voice of flesh, or the voice of enemy, the only difference is that the voice of bias compares different choices and seeks to express interest in one choice based on what is seen or perceived. This voice was at work in the life of Prophet Samuel when he sought to choose another son of Jesse over David - (So it *was, when they came, that he looked at Eliab and said, "Surely the LORD's anointed is before Him!" But the LORD said to Samuel, "Do not consider his appearance or height, for I have rejected him; the LORD does not see as man does. For man sees the outward*

*appearance, but the LORD sees the heart.) - 1
Samuel 16:6*

The voice of God and His Word are the surest way to
hear from the Lord. The goal of the enemy is to hinder
divine communication by leading to error or leading to
all other voices that are prone to error. Whenever you
are faced with the spirit of confusion when making a
decision for marriage, begin by meditating on the
following Scripture and the Lord will test out the word
to bring clarity.

> *"Beloved, do not believe every spirit, but test the
> spirits, whether they are of God; because many
> false prophets have gone out into the world. By
> this you know the Spirit of God: Every spirit that
> confesses that Jesus Christ has come in the flesh is
> of God, and every spirit that does not confess that
> Jesus Christ has come in the flesh is not of God.
> And this is the spirit of the Antichrist, which you
> have heard was coming, and is now already in the
> world."* **-1 John 4:1-3 NKJV**

Wrong Visions and Marriage Choices

Marriage is the only type of establishment where you
make choices and grade your own choices by your
experience. Many men listen to the voice of bias when

choosing a wife. As a general rule; if you have had sex with your wife-to-be before marriage, and you are seeking to pray to the Lord to determine whether she is your wife or not; you have a higher chance to receive a false vision or even dream. You will be seeing from your own imaginations, because you are already one with this individual. There is a spiritual concept taught in Jeremiah 29:8 where false diviners, false prophets cause people to see the wrong visions/dreams *"For thus says the LORD of hosts, the God of Israel: Do not let your prophets and your diviners who are in your midst deceive you, nor listen to your dreams which you cause to be dreamed.* This happens a lot when people are about to make choices, the enemy comes in false dreams to deceive.

False dreams or visions are made possible in marriage when there is a legal foothold into the soul. This usually happens during pre-marital sex. Any woman you have pre-marital sex with is already one with you in the soul, spirit and body. The Scripture found in 1 Corinthians 6:16 notes *"Or do you not know that he who is joined to a harlot is one body with her? For "the two," He says, "shall become one flesh." Whenever you have sex with a woman you are not married to, you become one with her.* If you are asking God if you should marry her, or if she is the one, because you are already living in sin, your stream is polluted, you will keep seeing her as thee one, even when she may not necessarily be the one. If you are having sexual intercourse with 3 women at the same time, you will be confused when you are asking the Lord which to marry because your soul, spirit is already fragmented, and visions become unclear, therefore, you will only see the one who is most dominant and has the strongest hold on you spiritually and in the soulish realm. And that one, may not be your God ordained wife. Therefore it is important not to get into sexual intercourse until marriage.

Other situations where you could see the wrong visions if you are making marriage choices.

- If you have been bewitched. Some unsaved women use witchcraft satanic methods to bewitch men into marriage proposals. A bewitched man will see wrong visions in their head.

Communications for Marriage

The first step in learning communication in marriage is by learning to hear Gods' voice. God is the Author of communication. When we learn to hear His voice, our skills become developed to learn to communicate in marriage, and communication is one of the lifelines of a marriage. Also, if you have lived a polluted life, seek the cleansing and deliverance of the Lord by going on a 3-day fast, and praying the Lord will purge you of all filthiness. Also, rededicate your life to the Lord Jesus, and do not return to sin. This is when the Lord will restore clear communication.

Prayers for Divine Communication

1. Father Lord, deliver me from the spirit of error at the gates of marriage set to lead me into wrong marriage choice, in the name of Jesus

2. Lord Jesus, deliver me from the spirit of confusion at the gates of marriage

3. Lord, deliver me from the spirit of lies and deception at the gates of marriage

4. Lord deliver me from false prophets and false prophecy at the gates of marriage

5. Lord, deliver me from the powers that deadens visions at the time of marriage in the name of Jesus

6. Father Lord, do not allow the enemy to steal my vision in the name of Jesus.

7. Lord Jesus, open my eyes that I may see deep secrets of your kingdom in the name of Jesus.

8. Lord Jesus, let the eyes of my understanding be open in the name of Jesus.

9. Father Lord, anoint my imaginations in the name of Jesus.

10. Father, anoint my mind to receive from You.

11. Father, wash my vision clean in the name of Jesus.

12. Lord, take away all filthiness and pollution hindering divine communications in the name of Jesus.

13. I shall not be deceived into marriage as Jacob was deceived into marriage.

14. I shall not lose my reasoning at the critical point of making marriage decisions.

15. I shall not be bewitched into the wrong marriage in the name of Jesus.

16. Lord, the spirit of deception shall not overtake me at the critical point of making marriage decisions, in the name of Jesus.

17. Lord, do not hide your face from me in the name of Jesus.

18. Lord, open my eyes that I may see your goodness as a man, in the name of Jesus.

19. Father, open my eyes and ears and mind, to make decisions grounded in you in the name of Jesus.

20. Lord Jesus, deliver my life and soul from fragmentation that came as a result of pre-marital sex, in the name of Jesus

21. Lord Jesus, deliver my life and spirit from the came as a result of pre-marital sex, in the name of Jesus.

22. Father, let your voice be audible to me as it was audible to Moses, in the name of Jesus.

23. Father, let your voice be audible to me as it was audible to Abraham in the name of Jesus.

24. Father, let your voice be audible to me as it was audible to Joseph, in the name of Jesus.

25. Father, let your voice be audible to me as it was audible to David in the name of Jesus.

26. Father, let your voice be audible to me as it was audible to the Lord Jesus.

Journal

Chapter 3

The Purpose of Marriage

We were taking a Marriage Readiness class with a couple who were about to get married, and they had no idea there were other purposes to a marriage than "loving each other and having children". Many older couples who have been in marriage do not have the privilege of this information too.

In this chapter, we dive into the purposes of marriage. The purpose of marriage is God's intention and plans for marriage. In other words, what He uses marriages to accomplish.

Every marriage under the right conditions - the right man marries the right woman and are united in faith has a purpose of God to fulfill. The purpose of a marriage is the original reason why God established a marriage, and the missions He has ordained that marriage to accomplish.

Purpose of Marriage #1: Marriage is one of the treasures of the kingdom of Heaven. God establishes marriage for couples to experience God's treasures on earth, as a shadow of the things to come. The husband fulfills this purpose by seeking to bring heaven's treasures into his marriage.

Purpose of Marriage #2: Marriage serves the purpose of symbolizing the relationship between Jesus Christ and the Church. Marriage is a reminder that as the man is the husband to his wife, Jesus is the Bridegroom, and the Church is the bride. The husband fulfills this purpose by emulating the character of Jesus.

Purpose of Marriage #3: Marriage is a prophecy of God's glory to be fulfilled. Marriage reminds us that God's glory is not to be shared with anyone.

Purpose of Marriage #4: In Marriage, it is possible for a man and woman to make a covenant which attracts God's approval. Marriage gives the opportunity for man and woman to bring their plans before God to advance their plan into a divine covenant.

Purpose of Marriage #5: Marriage involves the coming together of a man and a woman to fulfill a special assignment for God. One of the purposes of marriage is achieved when people come into a marriage and work together to further an agenda of God on earth

Purpose of Marriage #6: Marriage is for the bonding and alignment of man and woman to become strengthened to work together to glorify God, as the strength of one would be insufficient.

Purpose of Marriage #7: Marriage is the channel of the manifestation of the covenant of creation where children are born into the world, manifesting the mandate of fruitfulness.

Purpose of Marriage #8: Marriage is a God's ground for spiritual warfare needing the anointing of the husband and wife. God uses marriages to wage war against his enemies.

Purpose of Marriage #9: Marriage is the nurturing ground of destinies. Marriage is the ground for nurturing children who are ordained to fulfill God's purposes.

Purpose of Marriage #10: Marriage is worship unto the Lord. Where marriage is powered by the Holy Spirit, the couples are led to cultivating their marriage as worship to the Lord.

The purpose of marriage is vast! Marriage is the place of God's manifestations of His purposes, plans and will on earth. God uses marriages for preserving and instructing the world. Marriage is the smallest unit of the church; without marriage, the church will not stand. One of the core assignments of Jesus was to establish the church, after He had purchased the church. Looking at the verses below: Jesus had to be born and raised in a family where the marriage was intact. Looking at the importance of marriage, the angel of God came to resolve the controversy that threatened His mother's marriage prior to His birth.

Matthew 1:18-21 NKJV

> Now the birth of Jesus Christ was as follows: After His mother Mary was betrothed to Joseph, before they came together, she was found with the child of the Holy Spirit. Then Joseph, her husband, being a just man, and not wanting to make her a public example, was minded to put her away secretly. But while he thought about these things, behold, an angel of the Lord appeared to him in a dream, saying, "Joseph, son of David, do not be afraid to take to you Mary your wife, for that which is conceived in her is of the Holy Spirit. And she will bring forth a Son, and you shall call His name Jesus, for He will save His people from their sins."

The General Purpose of Marriage

There are several general purposes to marriages seen in the Scripture. In marriage, the mandate of fruitfulness, multiplication, filling the earth, subduing and having dominion is fulfilled (Genesis 1: 28). Marriages are the birthplace of destinies. Where children are raised within a marriage, destinies are preserved. Another purpose of marriage is companionship as seen in Genesis 2:18 which brings into existence the relationship between the husband and his wife. This mystery is a depiction of the relationship between Jesus Christ and the Church, and what is to come when the bride and the Bridegroom shall be joined together at the end of the day.

The general purpose of marriage is defined as the reasons why God established marriages; the assignments God uses marriage to accomplish. God's general purpose for marriage is for the display of God's kingdom, the unity of God, through the institution of marriage. God uses marriages to bring forth His treasures, to groom destinies and a place for worship unto God.

Every man needs to understand the general purpose of the marriage God is calling him into.

The One Flesh Mandate: When two unite as one flesh, they covenant to build further the general purposes of

God through their unity. The one flesh mandate sponsors the purpose of marriages. There is no general purpose until a couple unites as one. One flesh to build their lives, their children's lives, the community or any other purpose of God. A marriage built in the ways and the Word of the God serves as the ground for a solid society. God uses families to build the communities. Where families instruct on godly principles, the communities are established on solid values and are strengthened.

When two people are yet to marry, any man that has his ears opened by the Lord will be able to tell whether he has a purpose with this individual or not.

Prayer Sets for the Advancement of Your General Purpose in Marriage

1. Lord Jesus, empower me to fulfill your general purpose, in the name of Jesus

2. Lord Jesus, let my marriage be a fertile ground for your purpose in the name of Jesus

3. Father, let your general purpose of marriage not be defiled in my marriage, in the name of Jesus.

4. Father, my marriage shall not oppose your purpose in the name of Jesus.

5. Lord, reveal to me the spouse of my destiny that will work together with me to fulfill your purpose in the name of Jesus.

6. Your general purpose shall not be stolen from my marriage in the name of Jesus' name.

7. Father, let the purpose of my marriage be clear to me as the purpose of Isaac was clear to me in the name of Jesus.

8. Lord Jesus, reveal to me the purpose of my marriage.

9. Lord Jesus, give me a sound understanding of my purpose as a man in marriage.

10. Lord, reveal to me how to walk into my purpose in marriage, in the name of Jesus.

11. Lord Jesus, let my marriage be a delight to you, in the name of Jesus.

12. Lord Jesus, let my marriage be an acceptable worship offering to you, in the name of Jesus.

Journal

Chapter 4

Specific Purpose in Marriage

Each spouse has a specific purpose in marriage. When the specific purpose is determined, marriage moves faster into God's plan. In this chapter, we discuss the specific purposes of spouses in marriage. Love is one of the reasons people decide to go into marriage. Many times, when people get out of love, or stop loving each other, there is something left. A deeper love which is found in the purposes of God in each other.

> *Before I formed you in the womb, I sanctified you and I ordained you as a prophet to the nations.*
> **Jeremiah 1:5 NKJV**

The specific purpose of individuals in marriage is to be figured out before marriage. Love established in purpose is stronger than love without purposes. Love founded on purpose will outlive love which has no place for purpose. A man and a woman have a specific purpose in life and in marriage. Finding out the voice of God's assignment for your life.

What does God want to do through my life? This is where your unique voice and identity comes.

Specific Purpose of Marriage

Each marriage has a specific purpose, different from the general purpose. A specific purpose of a marriage is God's unique assignment for both couples that is permissible to be fulfilled only within the boundaries of their marriage, when planted in God's presence.

What is specific marriage purpose: Husband's Purpose + Wife Purpose = Specific marriage purpose

- **Adam's Purpose**: (One of the specific purposes of Adam was to tend and keep the garden of God) + **Eve's Purpose** (The specific purpose of Eve was to be a helper comparable to Adam in the garden) = **Specific Purpose:** (The specific purpose of their marriage was to tend the garden of God)

Understanding Specific Purpose of Spouse in Marriage

Each spouse has a specific purpose in marriage. When the purpose is found, then, they can both contribute to the general purpose of the marriage. Every spouse has a specific purpose in their marriage, and every marriage has a specific purpose unique to that marriage which is not the same as any other marriage.

The Husband's Specific Purpose: Your husband must have found their purpose before getting married to you. Just as the specific purpose of Adam was to tend the garden. He was ordained into this purpose before Eve came. It would be wrong for a man to state sex for reproduction and multiplication as their purpose. The specific purpose is the mission they have been called to execute for God on earth. When the man knows his purpose, his wife can help him, nurture his purpose. When the man does not know his purpose, the wife will help him find the wrong purpose that does not belong to him. Women are not designed to work with husbands without a purpose. Yet women are not called to help find their husbands their purpose. The husband must source out his purpose first, before getting married. In marriage, they can nurture and build together.

The Scripture below teaches that there is a purpose predestined. This purpose we are encouraged to search out prior to marriage.

> *In Him also we have obtained an inheritance, being predestined according to the purpose of Him who works all things according to the counsel of His will, that we who first trusted in Christ should*

be to the praise of His glory. **Ephesians 1:11-12NKJV**

The Wife's Specific Purpose: Women are companions, they are helpers, and amplifiers of great news. Every man has good news. The good news of every man is the purpose of God to be fulfilled through their lives. When a husband has found his purpose, women amplify the good news. When the husband fails to find his purpose, the woman becomes frustrated and finds him a purpose. Unfortunately, women are not given the mandate or permission to help identify their husband's purpose. However, a woman who is working in submission to the Lord, when she is yielded to the Holy Spirit, may be used to unlock her husband's purpose.

- Help the husband in fulfilling his purpose
- Manage the affairs of her household
- Intercede for her husband
- Help unlock the husband's purpose

The Unlocking of the Anointing: Women have the anointing to call forth the anointing of God out into action from their husband or children's life. They are anointed to place a demand on God's anointing upon the lives upon which they have a spiritual influence. The earlier women of the Scriptures were used to amplify the good news of resurrection, in the face of opposition and suppression of good news. Similarly, the words of a virtuous woman can unlock and build a man's purpose.

There are women who observe certain gifts in their husbands, and look for environments, influences, and people who can help these gifts blossom. They encourage their husbands to be around these influences.

The Silencing of the Anointing: Same way, a woman yielded to satan can silence the voice of the anointing of God upon whosoever they hold a spiritual influence, if allowed. This is why it is impossible for any man to succeed without the approval of his wife.

How the Voice of the Man's Anointing is Silenced

When your wife feels threatened by her friends' successes, and nagging at their husbands to be like their friends' husbands, if you conform and heed her voice, this is the beginning of abandoning your God-given voice to chase after shadows.

A woman is usually looking to assist your purpose. She gets idle when you have not found your purpose, and will seek to find one for you. Usually she cannot manufacture her husband's purpose, so she looks around for people working in purpose and pushes her husband towards that.

God uses certain people to build others up. If your wife is impatient, the devil may use her impatience to lure you away from your destiny helpers. These are the types of spirits at work in women whose husband is not yet in purpose, or who are on their way into purpose, and on a journey with the Lord. Your wife may demand that you leave a job where God is building you up. She may demand that you cut off a friendship that God is using to remold your life. This is the realm where there are other influences working through your wife's lives. We have worked with many couples; there was a trend God was showing us. The women loved the overall programs, and the way God was moving in their marriage. When it was time for God to address certain limitations upon a family coming from the women's side, some of these women had worked in witchcraft without telling their spouses, and that is holding down advancement; then the women manipulate their boyfriends to cancel the program, rather than completing and getting delivered. The Lord says, this is how the enemy reverses the anointing of the woman to silence the anointing of the man.

Fulfilling Individual Purposes in Marriage

The establishment of individual purposes to be carried out in the marriage. Marriage is ordained to support each other's purposes, not to kill it. Finding your purpose can be one of the quickest ways to hear God's voice when it comes to making marriage partner choices. God will never approve of a partner who will kill your purpose, or not support your purpose.

This is a tricky one though. You must be careful that the one you are evaluating whether they can support your purpose are fully equipped to do so; Not appearing to be able to support your purpose may not mean they are unable to, or that they cannot. So, you will need to press down in the Holy Spirit to find out.

The image you have of the person who can support your purpose may be totally different to what God has in mind. That individual may not even be where they are supposed to be. That does not mean they are not God's chosen for you!

The key point is this: God has for you a partner who matches and will help fulfill your purpose. They may not look like it at first. Meditate on the following:

> "And Samuel said to Jesse, "Are all the young men here?" Then he said, "There remains yet the youngest, and there he is, keeping the sheep." And Samuel said to Jesse, "Send and bring him. For we

will not sit down till he comes here." 12So he sent and brought him in. Now he was ruddy, with bright eyes, and good-looking. And the Lord said, "Arise, anoint him; for this is the one!" Then Samuel took the horn of oil and anointed him in the midst of his brothers; and the Spirit of the Lord came upon David from that day forward. So Samuel arose and went to Ramah.

1 Samuel 16: 11-13 NKJV

Spouses' Career in the Specific Purpose of Marriage

God has called spouses to unify as one, also in their careers. Your career and that of your spouse play a significant role in fulfilling God's specific purpose in your marriage.

The Story of Anna and John

When Anna and John met, John was a decorated government official with advanced education while Anna had a high school diploma and worked as an office secretary at an auto service center. John's family objected to their marriage with the concerns that Anna's professional background was no match to John's. John saw beyond Anna's current education level and profession. They weathered the storm and got married. In their first year of their marriage, Anna became a stay-at-home wife, got pregnant and they had their baby. Over the next 3 years, she was a stay-at-home mother, but interestingly, her career had grown. She studied online and completed her college degree in 3 years. She had also developed competencies in management. She worked with her husband to begin a family business. Their family business began to thrive, and it became clearer to John's family that he made the good choice. In this situation, the couples were able to align their careers into God's purposes for their marriage even though it did not seem like it at the beginning.

The Story of Bobby and Alice

Let's look at the life of Bobby and Alice. Alice was a consultant with a top Accounting firm. Bobby worked in Sales at a company which manufactured consumer goods. They looked like a good match and everything seemed great with their chemistry. Alice believed in working couples, Bobby had a background where there was only one breadwinner in the family, and the other spouse stayed home to support. Their wedding went well as friends and families came to offer support. Alice traveled 70% of the time, while Bobby worked in the same city as they lived. By their second year, they had their twins. Alice's work demands did not stay the same, it increased. Bobby resigned at his work to take care of the kids. He was not raised in homes where someone else watched the kids, and he preferred alternative roles where one spouse worked and the others raised the kids. Alice believed they needed to hire nannies to help assume babysitting roles while they both kept their jobs. This became a war in their marriage and the beginning of resentment. Alice's career continued to climb higher, while Bobby totally distanced himself from his career to spend more time raising their children. After their 8th year of marriage, Alice came home one day from a travel trip and shared the news that she has just been promoted as the COO (Chief Operating officer) of the company she worked for. Bobby despised this, knowing this would take away from their already-suffering family life. Alice thought Bobby was envious and felt threatened at her success, by the end of their 9th year of marriage, Alice filed for divorce. In this story, the couples seemed to be good matches at first, and their careers looked promising at the beginning, but things went awry immediately after the marriage began. This is common in many struggling families.

Aligning Careers

God has embedded the anointing in couples such that each of their anointing fuels the purpose of the other. Couples' career choices play a huge role in whether they'll fulfill God's specific purpose in their marriage or not. Some couples despise each other's career, while some work together. Couples who never work together, or have aligning careers, or careers that intersect at the core of their purpose will never enter God's specific purposes for their marriage.

Also, the enemy can hide under the "aligning career" rule to deceive, so beware. If you are a physician, your wife may not have to be a pharmacist to be a God ordained wife. Figuring this out is dependent on your communication with the Lord.

Career and Professional Improvements

Couples must be able to unify on all fronts. Where there is no oneness in purpose, it will be war for either of the spouses to make career or professional improvements. The mandate of oneness is also fulfilled when couples grow professionally together, thrive together in their academic pursuits, and help each other activate their calling, or unwrap their buried gifts. The husband is called to wash his wife and present her back to himself. unto you. This is the model Jesus gave. He's constantly cleaning the church, in and out, washing the church to make the church pure and holy, and become a standard fit for Him.

Finding God's Specific Purpose for You in Marriage

When couples meet, and planning to get married, we usually recommend that they define God's purpose for individual lives through a life mission statement. With a clearly defined purpose, marriage will not barely exist, but couples will live out God's purpose in bliss.

Divine purpose for establishment of individual purposes to be carried out in the marriage. Marriage is ordained to support each other's purposes, not to kill it. Finding your purpose can be one of the quickest ways to hear God's voice when it comes to making marriage partner choices. God will never approve of a partner who will kill your purpose, or not support your purpose.

This is a tricky one though. You must be careful that the one you are evaluating whether they can support your purpose are fully equipped to do so; Not appearing to be able to support your purpose may not mean they are unable to, or that they cannot. So, you will need to press down in the Holy Spirit to find out. It's God's plan to build the unique purposes of two people for His greater and special purpose in a marriage. God never shuts down the unique purpose of individuals just for them to fit into a marriage.

Understanding the Most Prominent Spirits in Women

There are three major spirits to learn about. The helpful spirit, the usurping spirit and the destroying spirit.

The **Helpful Spirit** helps her husband to fulfill his purpose. In doing that, her purpose is also fulfilled by God. Helpers will be used by God to help their husbands settle and become established into purpose.

The ultimate goal of any man looking to get married at the point of marriage is to pray and discern who the helper is.

- The helpful spirit will help the man nurture his purpose
- The helpful spirit will work with the man towards his God-given purpose

Action points:

- *Begin to find ways to help others around you. Help is merely a physical effort, but a spiritual state. People are helpful in their spirits first, and that help is translated into actions that blesses others.*
- *Set a goal to help a certain number of people each week*

The **Usurping Spirit** has no help to provide. The usurping spirit will use the husband to fulfill her agenda.

- A usurping spirit will use a man to get the Mrs. title, and that's it, that spirit goes back to the old ways of lawlessness and disrespect.
- A usurping spirit will destroy you and ruin your chances of getting into God's purpose.
- A usurping spirit will seek to marry for affluence, influence and name into a well-established family, not because she intends to help or because she has any good intention in marriage, but because she needs to be called by your family name, so she profiteer from that. The blessing of affluence, influence and good name should come to the right woman who is working in her calling as a helper.
- A usurping spirit does not look beyond the present moment, especially when you are just discovering your purpose.

A **Destroying Spirit** will destroy the man and hinder him from purpose. The devil's goal is to match men with women who will lure them out of their purposes. Therefore, men must be spiritually ready and have an open communication from God.

- When the man is supposed to be working towards your purpose, a destruction will spin up other irrelevant assignments to your purpose like causing, contention, and fights.

- A destroying spirit seeks to get married to get into careless spending and ruin the wealth you have built.
- A destroying spirit will tear down the man in words, and he will lose the will to do great things for God.

Understanding the Most Prominent Spirits in Women

There are three major spirits to learn about in this segment. The loving spirit, the usurping spirit and the destroying spirit.

The **Loving Spirit** in a man is revealed by his action, not by his words. He loves his wife, and he does everything to protect and shield her. He accepts her as his favor from the Lord.

How Does a Loving Spirit Manifest in the Husband?

Give give give...

1. Give her dedication to the Lord at all times. If you love her, give her back to the Lord all the time.
2. Give time to her: Spend time with her, she is your portion of vanity.
3. Give attention to her: Become attentive, she has deep spiritual insights, and the Lord will speak to you through her.
4. Give prayers: Give prayers concerning her.
5. Give honor: Honor her.

The **Usurping Spirit:** Women are called to be helpers, but men must not take advantage of that to manipulate women.

How Does a Usurping Spirit Manifest in the Husband?

Use use use...

1. A usurping spirit uses the woman to fulfill selfish needs and dump her.
2. A usurping spirit never sees a woman as valuable to your life.
3. A usurping spirit never loves the woman as yourself.

The **Destroying Spirit:** Men are called to protect, but a destroying spirit destroys a woman spiritually, financially, mentally and emotionally.

How Does a Destroying Spirit Manifest in the Husband?

Destroy destroy destroy...

1. A destroying spirit wreaks the emotion of the husband.

2. A destroying spirit wreaks the mental state of the husband

3. A destroying spirit abuses the husband verbally, mentally and every way possible.

4. A destroying spirit seeks to wreak the destiny of the husband.

Never allot the enemy to bring the spirit of destruction and taint your image as a man.

Prayer Sets for Special Purpose of God to be Revealed

1. Lord Jesus, visit my soul again like You did on the day you fashioned me

2. Lord Jesus, open to me the secrets to purpose

3. Father Lord, anoint my mind that my purpose will be made clear to me in the name of Jesus in the name of Jesus.

4. Father, reveal to me the specific purposes you have called me for, in the name of Jesus

5. Father, let my marriage be one filled with your purpose, in the name of Jesus.

6. Lord Jesus, fashion my marriage as one You delight to use for your purpose in the name of Jesus.

7. Father, my marriage shall not be one without reason or purpose, in the name of Jesus.

8. Lord Jesus, let me and my spouse understand your purposes for us beyond the shadow of doubt in the name of Jesus.

9. Father Lord, my marriage partner shall not swallow the voice of my purpose in the name of Jesus

10. Lord Jesus, I shall not choose the wrong partner for my marriage.

11. Lord, reveal my life purpose to me, in the name of Jesus.

12. Lord, reveal to me the helper of my purpose, in the name of Jesus.

13. Lord Jesus, purify me with your spirit, in the name of Jesus.

14. Thou powers of the destroyer shall not manifest within me in the name of jesus

15. Thou powers of the Usurping spirit shall not manifest within me in the name of Jesus.

16. Reveal to me the understanding of help in the name of Jesus.

17. Lord, reveal to me the helper of my purpose, in the name of Jesus.

18. Lord Jesus, You have called me an amplifier of good news, let my actions support this calling in my marriage, in the name of Jesus

19. Lord Jesus, take over my mind, let not my mind be in subjection to the powers of darkness in the name of Jesus.

20. Lord Jesus, let not my life be conducive for the powers of darkness in the name of Jesus.

21. Lord Jesus, send me amplifiers that would amplify my calling and purpose in the name of Jesus.

22. Lord Jesus, release words of good news to me, that I may amplify these words concerning my husband, in the name of Jesus.

Journal

Chapter 5

Understanding Roles in Marriage

Roles in marriages have spiritual impacts. Roles talk about the order and assignment of authority from God. The order in marriage is GOD - HUSBAND AND WIFE . God first, the husband submits to the Lord, and the wife submits to her husband. When the man understands and assumes her role, she gets full spiritual authority from God to work and function effectively in her role. When you depart from your role, which is your office of assignment in your marriage, the marriage loses the potency to forge ahead into purpose, and lives are at stake.

Assuming your God-given role will earn you the authority to lead in your marriage. Abandoning your God-given role is the fastest way for the enemy to take over any marriage. In this chapter, we discuss the roles in marriage. Many marriages crumble because roles were not understood by the couple. Maintaining roles in important to God, and we see this in the condemnation of the angels who left their domains in Jude 1:6 *"And angels who did not keep their own domain but abandoned their proper dwelling place, these He has kept in eternal restraints under darkness for the judgment of the great day".*

The Priestly Role of the Husband

The Husband is the head, the priest of the home, just like Jesus Christ is our great high priest. The perfect husband can be described as a Jesus-like model, powered by the spirit of love and one who carries the purpose of God. However, because of the imperfections of humans, people do not become the perfect spouse at the time of marriage, but they can work their way into this calling as written, "be ye perfect as your heavenly father is perfect ". The way to the husband's perfection is to conform to the image of Jesus and live in submission as Jesus did, "He is the *image of* the invisible God, the firstborn over all creation" as seen in Colossians 1:15. The route to perfecting the wife is shown in Ephesians 5:25-27 *"Husbands, love your wives, just as Christ also loved the church and gave Himself for her, that He might sanctify and cleanse her with the washing of water by the word, that He might present her* to *Himself a glorious church, not having spot or wrinkle or any such thing, but that she should be holy and without blemish".* The wife looking to become her best in her role, must submit and allow herself to be washed and to become the perfect wife.

The husband has the authority over every marriage and is ordained as the priest. The priestly authority is released upon the husband when marriage begins. This priestly authority is needed to bring his new family before the Lord, and to receive God's direction for the new purpose He is about to begin through them. Priests learn the ways of the Lord, hear from God and execute His missions. The husband when walking in His priestly calling downloads the vision for his family and leads his family right. A priest must lead by example. Leadership is one of the core skills a priest will need. Authority for leadership is also needed to influence the family. The first requirement for any man who desires to be anointed as the priest of God for his household is submission to the Lord. Authority is not acquired automatically, it also cannot be imposed, it is a gift from God given to those who live in absolute obedience to the Lord. As a general rule, when you fully submit to the Lord in every area of your life, He will measure out the authority to you and your wife will submit to you. If you live outside of submission, you have no valid authority in

God's presence, and He will not release authority to you.

The responsibility attached to priesthood is vast. Some is addressed in Exodus 28:11-12 where Aaron was charged with bringing the names of the tribes of Israel to God's presence. "With the work of an engraver in stone, *like* the engravings of a signet, you shall engrave the two stones with the names of the sons of Israel. You shall set them in settings of gold. And you shall put the two stones on the shoulders of the ephod *as* memorial stones for the sons of Israel. So, Aaron shall bear their names before the Lord on his two shoulders as a memorial" Similarly, the husband must bear the name of his wife, children and community, bringing them before the Lord at all times.

Understanding the Time Requirement to Perfection of Roles

1. It takes an average of 5 to 7 years for a man to become skilled in his role when it comes to leading her household.
2. It can take anywhere from 10 to 15 years for him to develop expertise in advanced leadership of her household.
3. Children who have the blessing of great parenting can save all these years and gain

experience by observing their parents, and bringing the good experiences into their own marriage.

4. Some men live 20 to 40 years through mistakes and learn their own lessons

The Route of Priesthood

1. Responsibility is the first step to priesthood in a marriage.

2. Living in absolute obedience to the Lord prepares the man for the journey of marriage.

3. When found faithfully as one who obeys, the authority of the Lord is released over the man

4. The anointing of priesthood is released upon the man to lead his family in the ways of God.

5. The priest loves and sets the example for his family to love.

6. Loving his wife, and identifying her as the favor of God for his life, and working together with her to build their marriage and nurture their children: A husband identifies his wife's calling as that of a shepherd, also known as a manager. The role of a manager is very prominent in a marriage. One of the examples we give about the helper's role is this; If you have so much money and you struggle with money management. You will need the services of a financial adviser to

understand how money works and how to multiply money. This is a similar role the Lord has called your wife to occupy.

Husbands, love your wives, just as Christ also loved the church and gave Himself for her, that He might sanctify and cleanse her with the washing of water by the word, that He might present her to Himself a glorious church, not having spot or wrinkle or any such thing, but that she should be holy and without blemish. So husbands ought to love their own wives as their own bodies; he who loves his wife loves himself. For no one ever hated his own flesh, but nourishes and cherishes it, just as the Lord does the church. For we are members of His body, of His flesh and of His bones. "For this reason a man shall leave his father and mother and be joined to his wife, and the two shall become one flesh." This is a great mystery, but I speak concerning Christ and the church.
Ephesians 5 : 25 - 32 NKJV

The Mantle of Leadership Releases Authority

The husband needs authority from God to lead his family. Leadership in marriage is impossible without the release of God's authority. This explains why many men find it difficult to lead their families in the way of the Lord. Leadership cannot be assumed without authority. Where does authority come from? Authority comes only from God. Some husbands impose authority on their wives when they perceive the lack of submission. This is a major sign that the husband has not submitted to the Lord or disobeyed the Lord at a critical spot in his marriage. Authority is not automatically acquired, and it cannot be imposed. It is attained through a deeper walk with the Lord. Authority comes as an anointing from God.   Every husband, who desires the anointing to carry authority in his family, needs to submit to God first.

The Priest's Leadership Duties

Leadership is one of the responsibilities of the husband. The proper execution of your leadership role as a husband will bring God's honor over your life. When the husband walks in his role, the honor of God is added to him, and this is the realm where the wife submits lovingly to her husband.

1. Lead his household in the ways of God.
2. Be responsible for the overall affairs of His household.
3. Bring His family before God's presence.
4. Love his wife.
5. Covers and intercedes for his wife in prayers.
6. Provides for his family.

The Perversion of the Priestly Role

The role of many husbands has been perverted because of perceived weaknesses. Husbands are ordained to lead, and should not allow wives to lead, as this was how Adam and Eve fell, and how Ahab and Jezebel fell out of God's presence. The husband must lead to retain the ordinance and covenant of God in that marriage.

Women have the shepherd anointing, which is also the manager's anointing. This anointing if not observed carefully can look like the priestly anointing but is not. The woman's anointing is for nurturing God's assignment placed in the care of her husband. The husband must not submit God's assignment to the leadership of the woman, but should allow the woman to help nurture, while he leads and directs the purpose. Whenever this happens, God's agenda upon that family is locked up, and the woman opens herself to curses.

Prayer Sets to Walk in Your Marital Role

1. Lord Jesus, let your will be done in my marriage.

2. Lord jesus,

3. Lord Jesus, open to me the secrets to purpose

4. Father Lord, anoint my mind that my purpose will be made clear to me in the name of Jesus in the name of Jesus.

5. Father, reveal to me the specific purposes you have called me for, in the name of Jesus

6. Father, let my marriage be one filled with your purpose, in the name of Jesus.

7. Lord Jesus, fashion my marriage as one You delight to use for your purpose in the name of Jesus.

8. Father, my marriage shall not be one without reason or purpose, in the name of Jesus.

9. Lord Jesus, let me and my spouse understand your purposes for us beyond the shadow of doubt in the name of Jesus.

10. Father Lord, my marriage partner shall not swallow the voice of my purpose in the name of Jesus

11. Lord, my calling shall not be perverted in marriage.

12. Lord Jesus, my calling in marriage shall not be desecrated in the name of Jesus.

13. Lord, let me not walk into condemnation by abandoning my domain in the name of Jesus.

Journal

Chapter 6

Knowledge Gaps in Marriage

The knowledge of spouse is one addressed in this chapter. We define and discuss knowledge gaps, examples and how to eliminate them. There are three levels of knowledge needed for marriage namely: *Primary knowledge, Spiritual knowledge and Soulish knowledge.*

Primary knowledge: This is the level where the knowledge of foundations, backgrounds, history, behavior is revealed. This level of knowledge is where pre-marriage couples usually hide a lot of information that is material to their marriage. They hide their lifestyles, debts, way of life, family foundations, past relationships and issues encountered.

Spiritual Knowledge: The Word of God helps provide access to spiritual knowledge. Spiritual knowledge provides insight into spiritual lives, spiritual foundation, and spiritual states.

- *Spiritual knowledge level 1:* Before marriage, they are getting a spiritual understanding of each other and growing in the knowledge of Christ together. For example, what is this person's spiritual standing before God? Where there is no spiritual knowledge founded in the Word of God, people advance into building a sexual life that destroys them. This is where transference of spirits, demon exchange and multiplication occurs. What is present in their lives spiritually? This level is only possible before marriage. We were praying for a mother. Her son was about to get married, and she wanted to pray for her son and his wife. The Lord said the wife to be was in witchcraft and needed to be delivered, or there will be trouble later in the marriage. She said they had been to a church to pray, and the woman is very experienced, she said no such thing. God said, tell them to go back to that place. When they went back to that place, she called to say, the woman minister said she saw it again but different this time, she said the bride-to-be was in a witchcraft group, but looks like she's turning her back to the group and about departing. The Lord said, warn them to not proceed into the marriage until she is delivered, if she wants deliverance. This realm of knowledge is supposed to be opened to people before marriage but is hardly ever open because of people's spiritual standing in God's presence. Everyone who will succeed in marriage should strive to understand the spiritual state of their spouse-to-be. Many people are marrying into the occultic without knowing. Any man of purpose must be spiritually alert, so that the enemy does not pair them with a satanist. Many men have been targeted and paired with satanists, who ensure all their lives that their husband's life is ruined.

- *Spiritual knowledge level 2:* They are advanced and learn that sexual experiences happen on a worship altar. They understand that sex is a spiritual activity, and in this realm, they are married and come to know each other sexually. Spiritual knowledge in faith helps them understand that sex is a spiritual activity that they use their body in carrying out. They go with the right spiritual foundation into this altar of their matrimony. This is the level where advanced spiritual knowledge of each other can be accessed, and it can only occur after marriage has taken place.

Soulish Knowledge: As seen in Psalm 139, the soul is the essence of man, and inside the soul is where the plans of the days of every man were written before they were born. The soul contains information about your purposes and special life assignments. The information in the soul is heavily guarded by the Lord. This is why the devil seeks to have access to this realm before marriage to figure out the purpose of men, and empty them of these purposes. This is why the Scripture in Proverbs 7:21-27 says to the men, "*With her enticing speech she caused him to yield, With her flattering lips she seduced him. Immediately he went after her, as an ox goes to the slaughter, Or as a fool to the correction of the stocks, Till an arrow struck his liver. As a bird hastens to the snare, He did not know it would cost his life. Now therefore, listen to me, my children; Pay attention to the words of my mouth: Do not let your heart turn aside to her ways, Do not stray into her paths; For she has cast down many wounded, And all who were slain by her were strong men. Her house is the way to hell, Descending to the chambers of death.* Many men who have fallen were not strong men. Strong men here denote men of great destinies. Any woman you are opened up to sexually automatically accesses your soul and the toolbox of your destiny which is housed in your soul. This is why the enemy is always going for the soul first, and the fasted way to do that is through pre-marital sex or sex outside of marriage.

In marriage, this is where the husband and wife become one ultimately, a place of revisitation of their marriage covenants before the Lord, a place where their purposes are revealed to each other, and where the two people become one. If this knowledge is opened to people pre-maturely, this is where curses and evil covenants are shared between people.

The Knowledge of Spouse

Adam had the perfect knowledge of his wife Eve from the time Eve was brought to him, after her creation. The Scriptures from Genesis 2: 21-23 note:

> And the Lord God caused a deep sleep to fall on Adam, and he slept; and He took one of his ribs, and closed up the flesh in its place. Then the rib which the Lord God had taken from man He made into a woman, and He brought her to the man. And Adam said: This is now bone of my bones And flesh of my flesh; She shall be called Woman, Because she was taken out of Man."

The man must have a deep primary knowledge of his wife-to-be, as they prepare to get into marriage. Adam knew she was taken from him. He knew this was the woman for him. The advanced knowledge of a spouse comes after the marriage, as seen in the Scripture in Genesis 4:1, "*Now Adam knew Eve his wife, and she conceived and bore Cain, and said, "I have acquired a man from the Lord".* This advanced knowledge is also known as sexual knowledge. Sexual knowledge should come only when the Lord has broken the barrier of all other types of knowledge in the pre-marital stage.

Spiritual knowledge is possible to a limited extent before marriage, but it advances even with marriage when couples hold a valid covenant before God and enjoy sexual experiences on God's altar upon their marriages. Where soulish knowledge precedes all other knowledge of spouse, there is limited opportunity available to know each other, and this creates what we define as knowledge gap. Knowledge gaps war against the design of God for couples to become one in their marriage. Knowledge gap creates a hole for the devil to reside in marriage. A dream marriage is only a fantasy when there is a knowledge gap and no workable action plan to close it.

What is the Knowledge Gap?

Knowledge gap, as the name implies, is a void of knowledge in a relationship. Knowledge is one of the resources required for building a strong marriage. When there is a knowledge gap, there is a part of your life or your partner's life that you are unaware of. Knowledge gaps can occur intentionally or unintentionally. Always, couples proceed into marriage based on the knowledge they have of themselves and their spouse. In doing this, they miss out on important information about each other, proceed with ignorance. Knowledge gap creates an invisible distance between couples. Knowledge gap usually exists when sexual knowledge has occurred, where couples only meet in the soulish and spiritual realm without understanding or knowing the everyday reality or background of each other, or the activities that guides their lives.

Knowledge Gap Examples

For example, one of the couples had a history of kickstarting their sexual life with pornography. This has caused uncontrollable sexual urge in the times past and has landed them in a lot of trouble including getting involved in incest with a sibling. Now healed, and about to get married. Leaving this important piece of information out creates a huge gap that must be closed to strengthen the marriage. Both parties should come together to identify this gap, as they are becoming one flesh.

John and Joanna are about to get married, John's mother is controlling, overprotective and has possessed her children's marriages. John is the last son. John's older brothers faced a hard time because of their mother's behavior, and their marriages have suffered as a result. John is afraid to inform Joanna about his mother's attitude.

If John and Joanna proceed without this information getting across to Joanna pre-marriage, Joanna will meet with the shock of her life because she perceives John's mother to be the best mother-in-law she cannot wait to have.

- Knowledge gaps could be a debt that is not disclosed before marriage.
- Knowledge gaps could be an ongoing relationship that is not disclosed before marriage.
- Knowledge gaps could be a child born out of wedlock that was not disclosed before marriage.
- Knowledge gaps could be a major event that is material to a marriage that was kept secret.

When trying to determine whether withholding an information constitutes a knowledge gap. You can ask, "is this information intentionally withheld?

Becoming Vulnerable and Secured in Your Spouse

By becoming vulnerable to one another, couples become one, understanding each other's fears, desires, weaknesses, strengths, abilities, wants, and needs. The place of vulnerability is the place of no shame where the covenant of one flesh is fulfilled. As you are looking to open and expecting the same, you must open up yourself completely without reservation. As your partner opens themselves, there must be no disdain, blame or shaming of your partner.

Consequences of Keeping Knowledge Gaps Open

Many men or women never get delivered from shame and they will never fully open certain knowledge to their spouse or spouse-to-be. The knowledge of a spouse is so crucial that you cannot miss it or allow any gap in your marriage because you become one.

- If your spouse used to be a witch and she did not disclose this to you. In marriage her former witchcraft life will hunt you both, and you will be in a warfare you know nothing about.

- If your spouse aborted multiple pregnancies and she did not tell you, in marriage, you will have to deal with the cry of vengeance crying against you both, and you will fight bitterly against the spirit of poverty.

- If you impregnated 10 women and sponsored all 10 into abortions. If you hide this from your wife, she will be fighting a war she knows nothing about, and it is impossible to win.

- If you were in the occultic and you did all forms of rituals and you did not tell your wife, she will be a partaker when the voice of blood cries against your family and it will be difficult for her to know where the affliction is coming from.

Closing Knowledge Gaps

Knowledge gaps create walls and build boundaries between couples, that only time will uncover. Closing all knowledge gaps will set the ground rolling for authentic communications required for our body, soul and spirit to become one. Knowledge gaps can be very difficult to close as those who withhold knowledge may fear or live in shame. Follow this way to work on closing your knowledge gaps prior to marriage.

1. Maintain a godly and positive attitude when your spouse-to-be shares knowledge with you.

2. If you are the one with information to share, keep up your spirit, and prayerfully disclose information to them.

3. Set the goal of closing the knowledge gaps so that you can both overcome every challenge that comes your way that seeks to hide in darkness.

4. Share or receive all information with thanks. Never feel entitled to that information.

5. Consider all sides of the information shared.

6. Consider the implications of the information shared.

Limiting the Risks of Knowledge Gap

Knowledge gap is usually easier to close when there is awareness of the information hidden. Where there is no awareness, knowledge gaps could exist, and one of the parties end up living in regret or feeling cheated. You can check if you risk any knowledge gap to minimize the risks. No two marriages are ever the same, and no two marriages will ever be built the same. People are different, God's purposes for people are different.

Prayer Sets for God's light and knowledge upon Marital Life

1. Light of Israel, reign over my marital life, in the name of Jesus.

2. Light of Israel, shine your lights into every area of my life, in the name of Jesus.

3. Light of Israel, shine your lights into every area of my spouse-to-be's life, in the name of Jesus.

4. Light of Israel, reveal the knowledge of the Lord Jesus over my marital life in the name of Jesus.

5. Light of Israel, let the ancient secrets that hold the key to a godly marriage be opened unto me in the name of Jesus.

6. Lord, let me see your light in my marriage, in the name of Jesus

7. Lord, let your light overshadow my marriage in the name of Jesus.

8. No hiding place for the enemy in my marriage in the name of Jesus.

9. Lord, let the face of your countenance shine upon my marriage in the name of Jesus

10. The glory of my marriage shall not enter darkness, in the name of Jesus

11. Lord Jesus, shine your light upon my spirit and the spirit of my spouse, in the name of Jesus.

12. Lord Jesus, shine your light upon the soul.

13. Lord, open my spiritual eyes in the name of Jesus.

14. Father, cleanse me where I am fidelity in the name of Jesus.

15. Father, deliver me from all forms of uncleanliness in the name of Jesus.

16. Father, open my eyes to see the hidden things that will bring me into my marital destiny in the name of Jesus.

17. Father, open my ears to hear the hidden signs that will bring me into my marital destiny in the name of Jesus.

18. Father, do not hide your face from me concerning marriage in the name of Jesus.

19. Lord Jesus do not let me enter the trap of the enemy concerning marriage in the name of Jesus.

20. My Lord and My Father, do not let me enter into the snare of satanists in the name of Jesus.

21. Lord Jesus, I shall not be deceived into fleeing away from the rightful spouse of destiny in the name of Jesus.

22. Lord Jesus, I shall not be deceived into making the wrong choices in the name of Jesus.

23. Let the knowledge of Jesus expose all perverted knowledge that the enemy seeks to bring my way to deceive me in the name of jesus.

24. Let the knowledge of Jesus work with my mind in the name of Jesus, to be able to make sound decisions in the name of Jesus.

25. Let the knowledge of Jesus expose all that is in me that I seek to hide from my spouse, but will cause us disaster in our marriage, in the name of Jesus.

26. Let the knowledge of Jesus expose all that is hidden in my spouse that will cause a disaster in our marriage in the name of Jesus.

27. Lord, let your healing be complete in us as the knowledge gap is closed in the name of Jesus.

Journal

Chapter 7

Finances for Marriage

Finance is one of the strongest resources that marriage runs on. Every couple must forecast the monthly financial need and how it is going to be met prior to getting married. The lack of finances is a major road blocker to God's purposes in marriage through couples. This chapter discusses finances as one of the gateways to a blissful marriage.

Many purposes of a marriage will succeed if the financial need to further that purpose is met. When finances are not in order, marital purposes and goals can be ruined. One of the dangers to new marriages is financial baggage. Financial baggage, when brought into a new marriage, pulls down the marriage instantly.

Therefore, every man after God's heart must husband finances for marriage and plan to meet this need prior to getting married.

But if anyone does not provide for his own, and especially for those of his household, he has denied the faith and is worse than an unbeliever.

1 Timothy 5:8 NKJV

Determining Marriage's Financial Need

Every marriage is built differently and called for unique purposes. Some marriages will require greater financial resources to begin strongly while others will require less to succeed, depending on the current financial positions of the potential spouses. The husband needs to understand the financial need of the average marriage by considering the daily living expenses before making commitments to a marriage. Many men have committed to marriage in ignorance and refuse to take responsibility once the marriage begins. This begins many sorrows for such men.

Every husband holds a spiritual authority. That authority is lost where the husband steps down from his role of providing for his household. When the wife takes up financial responsibility the husband opens himself to the chains of financial lack which the enemy uses to hold captive husbands who are not walking in their authority.

When the Woman Must Not Assume Financial Responsibility.

The wife-to-be must assess the husband's ability to provide the basic necessity of life for the new family in marriage, or his plans to do that. When the bride-to-be takes up a future financial responsibility, she locks herself into an unending chain. This implies "buying the favor of the man to get him to marry you". You can never really know if a man will do anything legally possible to marry you, if you sponsor his lack when you are not married to him.

- God has not authorized the unmarried woman to bear financial responsibility of a man
- It is not the woman's duty to sponsor her husband to marry her.
- The woman should not purchase her wedding ring that will be presented to her.

These financial commitments are highly spiritual and when the woman gets into the man's role, it constitutes role perversion and earns her a curse of slavery, and places them in bondage.

When the Woman May Intercede for Her Husband

After marriage has occurred, the woman can share financial burdens with her husband in the management of the household, but the responsibility of the household must not be forcefully passed on to the wife. Heaven's design is that the husband provides for his family's basic necessities of life. After their marriage, if the wife is doing well financially, she can choose to assist her husband, even if he is doing well financially. The virtuous woman described in Proverbs 31 was a merchant, an international trader who had sufficient and provided for her household.

Prepare a Place : The Man's Duty

As couples get closer to marriage, the husband must have moved to the expected income level he will be bringing into his new family. Men are called to prepare a place suitable for marriage. This is found in Jesus' Word as He departs the world to go prepare a place ahead. The world is changing, and the enemy has deceived many women into preparing a place for a man to live. Many women will do anything to lure a man into a marriage, including opening their doors to him.

> And if I go and prepare a place for you, I will come again and receive you to Myself; that where I am, there you may be also.

John 14:3 NKJV

Preparing a place also ties into the man's role as the priest, the leader and the head of the household. The head of the household does not become the squatter in the household. When men move in with women, their spiritual authority and cover is taken away, and the covenant of lack and hardship sets in. They are relegated into hardship and hard toil, because they have abandoned their position in God's presence.

Indicators of Financial Unreadiness:

You can access your financial readiness for marriage using the following measures.

- Men unable to afford a home and living with the bride-to-be
- Relying on the bride-to-be for finances
- Having no financial plans or sources of income.
- Have you itemized the daily cost of maintaining a family if you get married?

Daily Living Expenses

You will also need finances to maintain your household! Couples separate over this. Where there is no understanding of associated costs of running a home, a breadwinner may wake up to a different reality after marriage and throw the ball. Here are popular costs you should remember to add to your plans.

- *Home*
- *Food*
- *Transportation (Car, insurance, service)*
- *Electricity*
- *Water*
- *Gas*
- *Subscriptions/Cable: You will need to pay cable bills monthly*
- *And even more, diapers, baby food, clothes, wipes, toys, healthcare, clothing when the kids arrive.*

Financial Considerations

Financial considerations must be made before marriage. The man is in the right position to bring this forward, putting all considerations into a discussion and well documented place so that you are in the same shoes. Considerations will vary, but they must occur and be well-managed. Considerations must go beyond the daily living expenses highlighted above, as this is only the basics.

Managing Money

Money management skills are one of the factors that will lead to a healthy or unhealthy financial life in any marriage. Couples must think of how they will manage money. These days, there are many financial management services. This is a very important consideration.

Financial Balance

Marital Financial Balance is the balance couples must find in their finances when they get into marriage. Where there is a marital financial imbalance, there is heavy weight on either side of the scale, the end of the scales representing both spouses.

Marital Financial Equilibrium is the perfect spot where couples' finances are in a stable weight on the scale. This is achieved when couples do not allow forces to place unnecessary weight on their finances.

Marital Financial Imbalance occurs when one or either of the couple has carried weight such that there is imbalance on their financial scale.

(Marriage Financial Balance and Marriage financial Equilibrium, Marital Financial Imbalance are marriage terms)

Talking about budget, when two people meet, they come from different backgrounds. We worked with a couple who came from different opposing backgrounds. One was raised in luxury, the other was raised in lack, they were married. One of them had major problems living life on a budget, while the other one lived a life of budget.

Budgeting is a process of allocating resources to upcoming needs, and setting a cut-off point to which resources can no longer be used. With budgeting, you have a clear picture of what you can spend from your income, cut out unaffordable expenses and see if there is the need to generate more income. Every couple should embrace budgeting. Couples who consider the Scripture - Luke 14:28 - "*For which of you, intending to build a tower, does not sit down first and count the cost, whether he has enough to finish it*" will not fall into financial ditches resulting in living life without the use of budget.

Finance and Wedding

The wedding event is one of the top times in couples' lives where financial imbalance occurs. The wedding day is a day like no other. It is a special day and should be celebrated. Your wedding day should however not set your finances in disarray or put you on a downward spiral as you begin your marital life. As a rule, wedding budgets must not bring baggage into marriage. The man with the heart of God must not allow his finances to be pressurized to fund large-sized wedding events with big budgets they cannot afford, or that will hurt the future finances in their marriage.

Shifting into Financial Oneness From "Me" to "Us"

One of the first lessons couples we share under this segment is becoming one in finances. The more unity in finances, the more financial freedom a marriage has. In marital finance, couples cannot individualize finances, they must unite as one to work in God's ordinance of oneness for marriage.

Prayer Sets for God's Abundance in Marriage

1. Light of Israel, shine your light upon my marital finance, in the name of Jesus.

2. Lord Jesus, open unto me, the revelation of finances in marriage, in the name of Jesus.

3. Father, let my marital finances be ordered into your ways, in the name of Jesus.

4. Lord, release the gifts and skill for sound financial management upon me and my spouse in the name of Jesus.

5. The enemy shall find no void in our finances to afflict my marital finance in the name of Jesus.

6. Our marital finance shall not be a reproach in the name of Jesus.

7. Our marital finance shall bring honor to the name of the Lord.

8. Lord Jesus, let my mind be the mind of Jesus concerning finances in marriage in the name of Jesus.

9. Lord Jesus, deliver me from processes that lead into financial bondage in the name of Jesus.

10. Lord Jesus, equip me to stand up in your authority to make financial decisions that will be beneficial to my marriage according to the will of the Lord, in the name of Jesus.

11. Lord Jesus, equip me to flee from all temptations of financial decisions that will bring poverty into my marriage in the name of Jesus.

12. Lord Jesus, close all doors and habits that imports the spirit of poverty into marriage in the name of Jesus.

13. Lord Jesus, close all doors that imports the spirit of economic slavery into marriage in the name of Jesus.

14. Lord Jesus, deliver me from the spirit that leads men into decision-making by emotions in the name of Jesus.

15. Lord Jesus, let my decision making be guided by your Word in the name of Jesus.

16. Lord Jesus, deliver my marriage from ungodly influences that seek to lure into poverty in the name of Jesus.

17. Lord Jesus, deliver the mind of my spouse from consumerism in the name of Jesus.

Journal

Chapter 8

Spiritual Readiness for Marriage

The spiritual state of a couple determines their spiritual readiness for marriage. Marriage is spiritual, and couples must come in spiritually prepared to navigate its spiritual complexities. The more couples allow Jesus Christ to grow and dwell in them, the more prepared they become for marriage. Spiritual readiness refers to the state of the husband conforming to the image of Jesus, ready to commit all his ways to the Lord, give the best to his wife, and his preparedness to wash his wife with the Word of God. The spiritual readiness of a woman for marriage can be determined by willingness to completely yield and submit to the Lord, her husband and be washed by the Word of God so she can be presented back to her husband.

Marriage and Faith

The common grounds for couples in marriage is their faith. Where couples have both accepted Jesus Christ as love and savior, there is a common ground to build every other thing on. Unequal yoke is a state where one spouse is of another faith, and one has come to the acceptance of the Lordship of the Lord Jesus. Spiritual problems are usually potent and hard to resolve where couples are not of the same faith because there is no congruence in belief and in the mindset. Therefore, we ask these questions when couples are about to get married to research the spiritual background of each other to determine whether both parties have Jesus as their Lord. If you marry an unsaved spouse, God may work on them and change them, but this is not guaranteed. Many have made the mistake of waiting for their spouse to convert and have entered a lifetime of contention due to difference in faith.

Is Your Spouse-to-be Really Saved? The current spiritual life of your spouse will help or limit you from getting closer to your marital status. Their relationship with the Word of God and whether they live out the Word of God can tell you about their relationship.

Marriage and Covenants

Marriage is a form of covenant. Covenants are spiritual contracts. Spiritual contracts require spiritual awareness, attentiveness, maturity to fulfill. When couples get married, they enter the covenant of oneness, which opens a higher realm of oneness in all types of contracts that each spouse is a part of, good or evil.

Marriage is a covenant with other sub-covenants in existence. Every marriage has at least 4 types of covenants. It could be more depending on the type of foundation each of the spouse is coming from:

#1 *Covenant between God and the Couple:* This is the covenant of marriage ordained by God, established between a couple and the Lord. Every type of marriage established is covenant to the Lord. This is the agreement with God as a witness, where the Lord marks two people as married, and keeps their covenant. Whether two people are ordained to be marital partners or not, whenever two people enter the covenant of marriage, the Lord seals it, and that marriage becomes valid in God's presence.

#2 *Covenant of Purpose:* There is a sub-covenant formed also in marriage. This covenant is the covenant where two people become partners in the purpose of God.

Under these covenants are children born. Under this covenant is the covenant of purpose each spouse fulfilled. However, there is a caveat to this covenant - when people marry the wrong spouse that is not ordained of God, this covenant is not accessed. Because of this covenant, the kingdom of darkness seeks to align many with the wrong spouses, so they can annul this covenant in the lives of people with great destiny.

#3 Covenant between and One of the Parties in the Marriage: This covenant goes into a marriage where one of the parties getting married had a prior and active covenant that they would get married to an ex-boyfriend or girlfriend. This is one of the most dangerous types of covenant to stick to people as they enter marriage. Covenants with past sexual partners if not broken is a timebomb in marriage. Sexual covenant is not instantly broken until personal deliverance is sought. It becomes more dangerous because one of the parties getting married does not inform the other when they were supposed to have meaningful conversations, unfortunately, this covenant affects not only one part, but the couple, and the entire future they intend to build.

#4 Existing Family Covenants: These are family covenants (godly and ungodly) which exist in families

where people marry. When parties marry their spouses, they also inherit those covenants through marriage. Some of these covenants are well-hidden, especially the evil ones. When parties go into marriage, they suddenly realize certain patterns begin to appear after marriage. Therefore, many people say their spouse changed after marriage. The reason is because there were underlying covenants in the family you married into, or in your family that is activated through marriage. If the family you married worships an idol and expects everyone marrying into that family to worship the same idol, but you are a child of the Living God. You will have to break that covenant over your life and marriage, otherwise, the idol will demand worship from you in many ways, through different manifestations of trouble. When not properly addressed, certain covenants begin to demand for spiritual repayments from the spouses or their children.

There are also covenants existing if there are previous marriages, or previous children outside of wedlock.

Marriage and Spiritual Threats

The most successful marriages face severe attacks from the devil. Understanding why the devil wages war against marriages can motivate couples to grow spiritually. Satan hates marriages, and wars against marriages spiritually. The following article explains why satan sends his best against marriages and why couples should pursue spiritual growth prior to marriage. Satan attempts to fight everything that has the name of God on it. The devil tries hard to fight every marriage and will attempt to fight yours too. Here is why.

1. Marriage is a prophetic act.
2. The marriage between the Lamb of God and His bride will precede in the season where Satan will be chained for 1000 years.
3. The devil is fearful of marriages, being remembered that every marriage ordained by God on earth is a look alike of the heavenly marriage to take place just before his destruction
4. The Church (The bride of Jesus) will be reunited to Jesus in person since the institution of the Holy Communion in the most beautiful marriage supper that we would ever experience in heaven.

Marital Spiritual Balance

Marital Spiritual Balance is where husband and wife are pursuing spiritual growth very close to the same level. They have a spiritual balance, and one can support each other spiritually in prayers.

Marital Spiritual Imbalance occurs when one or either of the couple has no spiritual life that can accommodate the spiritual demands of their marriage. Hence, the spiritual weight falls on one of the couples to bear.

Marital Spiritual Covers: Husbands and wives are called to protect each other spiritually from the powers of darkness. Where the husband prays for the wife, the husband covers his wife, and goes to the Lord on behalf of her, and the same applies to the wife. The wife can cover her husband spiritually.

Common Spiritual Wars in Marriage

Marriages fight different types of war. In this segment we discuss the common ones.

Demonic War: This is a war brought in through demons. The demon of masturbation and pornography bring in discontentment to sex lives of couples. Demonic wars can also manifest when demons take over the affairs of a household through the spirit of lust, anger, rage and violence in the household.

The Sexual Perversion War: The scripture taught in 1 Corinthians 7: 2 "Nevertheless, because of *sexual* immorality, let each man have his own wife, and let each woman have her own husband". One of the primary reasons for marriage is to avoid sexual immorality. Sexual immorality occurs when there is an ongoing sexual perversion war.

Sexual perversion occurs when sexual inclinations are channeled wrongly, whether to the wrong individuals, objects, thoughts or imaginations. Many marriages suffer from the sexual perversion war as the enemy gets the husband to seek out sexual pleasures from pornography, masturbation, or with the wrong individual.

Unholy Covenant: Strange covenants in the couple's foundations can embattle a marriage spiritually. Witchcraft covenants, family idol worship, unbroken past covenants with former lovers, unfulfilled marriage promises to past exes are covenants that allow the devil to rage freely in marriages.

The Wedding Day Warfare: The wedding day is a major day of target for the enemy to wreak havoc. In the book, Evil Participants in Marriage, we discussed 8 common satanic devices deployed at weddings by the devil. The wedding is a day of access to the couple and opportunities for the enemy to strike during their unguarded moments. Some wedding practices are satanic worship disguised in fun, some are idol rituals, like putting and rubbing certain types of ointment on the bride, feet washing with bewitched water in some countries, broom jumping and many others. We recommend for couples not to consent to any rituals not founded in the Word of God during their wedding ceremonies.

The Armor of God in Marriage

Marriages fight different types of war. In this segment we discuss the common ones. As found in Ephesians 6:10-11 "*Finally, my brethren, be strong in the Lord and in the power of His might. Put on the whole armor of God, that you may be able to stand against the wiles of the devil*", the armor of God in marriage shields the couple away from all sorts and sizes of spiritual attacks.

Understanding the ways of the marital enemy: The marital enemy is one who stands against the essence of marriage, seeking to distort the purposes of God through the demolition of a marriage. Marital enemies are spirits inhabiting people. The Scripture reminds in Ephesians 6: 12- 13 "*For we do not wrestle against flesh and blood, but against principalities, against powers, against the rulers of the darkness of this age, against spiritual hosts of wickedness in the heavenly places. Therefore, take up the whole armor of God, that you may be able to withstand in the evil day, and having done all, to stand.*

The word of God gives guidelines to putting on the armor of God in marriage.

- #1: A marriage must be founded on 100% truth. No secrets, no hidden agendas, both spouses must be congruent and unite in the soul, spirit and body. "Stand therefore, having girded your waist with truth, having put on the breastplate of righteousness"
- #2 Couples must understand that their marriage is for the purpose of the gospel of the Lord Jesus, and the symbol of a prophecy awaiting manifestation.
- #3 Couples must be filled with faith, with full assurance that the Lord will always come through regardless of what the enemy throws at them
- #4 Couples must guard their soul with the Word of God and hold onto the salvation they have received firmly.

#5 The couple must be filled with the holy-spirit and live a life of worship and prayers.

Accepting Your Wife as God's Favor in Marriage

Every man who finds a wife obtains favor from the Lord; the Scripture teaches. When you find a wife, that's your favor from the Lord. This is also spiritual. God's favor is released to man who accepts and joyfully receives his wife as his favor from the Lord and cherishes her. We ministered to a man who has lost his job and was struggling to find an economic balance in life. The Lord says, ask him where his wife is, he says, they live in the same house but hardly talk. God says, tell him, "**I will release my blessing upon him the day he accepts and treats his wife as his favor**". Some men, especially when they have multiple options prior to marriage and finally choose one, get the "marriage remorse" where they feel they chose the wrong spouse after marriage. They begin to misbehave towards the wife. The Scripture notes in Proverbs 30:21-23 - "*Under three things the earth shakes, and under four it cannot stand: Under a servant when he becomes king, under a fool when he is filled with food, under a woman who is not loved when she gets a husband, and under a woman servant when she takes the place of the woman of the house*". There are covenants of God that defend the unloved wife. This covenant was manifested in Leah, Jacob's wife as seen in Genesis 29:31 "When the LORD saw that Leah *was* unloved, He opened her womb; but Rachel *was* barren". There is the covenant of barrenness or lack unleashed upon a man and whatever he holds precious when he is not loving towards his life. The Lord closes the door to all forms of fruitfulness.

Prayer Sets for Godly External Relations and Destruction to Deadly Influences

1. Lord Jesus, overshadow our marriage, and become the driver of our marriage.
2. Lord Jesus, protect the gates of my marriage with your fire, in the name of Jesus
3. Lord Jesus your Spirit lead into profitable external revelations in the name of Jesus
4. Lord Jesus. Shield your marriage from the powers and devices of darkness used to destroy marriages in the name of Jesus.
5. Lord Jesus, shield our marriage from the wicked powers of the evil participants in the name of Jesus.
6. Lord Jesus, shield our marriage from the curse of uncleaving in the name of Jesus.
7. Deliver my marriage from the handwriting of darkness in the name of Jesus.
8. Lord Jesus, deliver my mind from the insecurity in the name of Jesus.

9. Lord Jesus, I shall not close the door towards my destiny helpers in the name of Jesus.

10. Lord Jesus, insecurity from within my spouse shall not close the door towards my destiny helpers in the name of Jesus.

11. Lord Jesus, I receive the mind of Jesus in my external relations in the name of Jesus.

12. Lord Jesus, let all relations be in your Word and in your Way in the name of Jesus.

Journal

Chapter 9

External Relations in Marriage

A marriage must exist as a unity between husband and wife, while maintaining healthy godly relationships with friends, families and others that are not part of the marriage. In this section, we define external relations and external relationships.

Marital External Relations: This is the way couples interact with people outside of their union. External relations can be temporary. External relations can be a blessing, if done well, and can become a curse to a marriage if done incorrectly.

Marital External Relationships: This is more about the nature of associations which couples form with people outside of their union. External relationships lean towards the long-term. Similarly, external relationships can bring blessings, or troubles to marriages, depending on the modalities.

External Relations and External Relationships

External relations and relationships co-exist together. For example, there will be interaction between a couple and their friends. The interaction is how they relate, and the friendship is their relationship.

Marriage & The Ordinance to Become One Flesh

Married couples have a mandate from God - TO BECOME ONE FLESH. In the earliest days after the creation of man, God gave the ordinance of marriage in Genesis 2:24 *"Therefore a man shall leave his father and mother and be joined to his wife, and they shall become one flesh"*. This mandate faces major challenges, as the devil seeks to bring destruction to this mandate.

There is an ordinance of God in marriages that the devil is actively defying today. Concerning all marriages, God decreed that there must be such unification of the man and the woman that they become one flesh. For a man and woman to unite as one in flesh, this simply means their mind, soul and spirit has become one, considering that the body is the container where the soul, mind and spirit resides. From the beginning of marriages, satan has been resisting this oracle of God and he continues to do that today. The enemy is defying this oracle of God by bringing shame and disgrace into marriages.

The Role of Evil Participants in Marriage

In deliverance ministry, God has shown us tons of satanic modes of afflicting marriages. Many marriages have been chained under the wrong external relations and relationships. Satan was the first evil participant in a marriage ever reported. The marriage of Adam and Eve had been newly established, and they were living in the word of God. Satan, an evil participant, came along to lure them out of their life inside the protection of God's words, and they became exposed to death. Ever since this incident, the devil has mass recruited agents, reproduced evil participants, and sent them out into the world to introduce toxins into marriages to afflict couples and crumble marriages.

An evil participant is assigned to tear apart and ensure couples never become one flesh. An evil participant is an individual powered by the forces of darkness with the sole agenda of ensuring that husband and wife never become one. An evil participant goes into marriages to uphold wicked ordinances that have gone out in the kingdom of darkness against a marriage. The role of an evil participant is to set up an operation within a marriage to tear down God's altar in that marriage. If an evil participant is running their operations in your marriage, you cannot become one flesh in your marriage regardless of how long you have been married or how promising your marriage seemed before you got married. When an evil participant is at work in a marriage, satan is already in that marriage. An evil participant distorts the reasoning of their captives such that the captive is unable to reason in God's Word anymore. Due to the extent of damage an evil participant can bring into marriage, many husbands or wives are rightfully extra protective of their marriages. Therefore, God calls for the man to be sensitive spiritually to the wiles of the enemy.

Gateway of External Relations

Gateways are the gate keeping principles you set up with the Word of God found in Philippians 4:8 ("Finally, brothers and sisters, whatever is true, whatever is noble, whatever is right, whatever is pure, whatever is lovely, whatever is admirable—if anything is excellent or praiseworthy—think about such things"). Every couple must bring every external relationship through the following lenses to determine whether such relations are good for them?

The Husband's Guide to Understanding External Relations

On external relations, marriage elevates the relationship between the husband and his wife into a bond stronger than any other earthly relationships.

Therefore a man shall leave his father and mother and be joined to his wife, and they shall become one flesh.
And they were both naked, the man and his wife, and were not ashamed - Genesis 2:24

RULE 1: The husband must be willing to leave relationships, even the closest parental relationships to cleave and become one with his wife.

RULE 2: The husband must be willing to be transparent and vulnerable to his wife, without shame.

External Relationships and Marriage

External relationships are needed and may be used by God to build, strengthen and promote God's mission in a marriage. The devil also attempts to use external relationships to tear apart, weaken and destroy God's purposes for marriage. Couples need to relate with people outside marriage in everyday life. All relations must be pure, healthy and must lead closer to God. In the next segment, we discuss the main types of external relations a couple would have during the lifecycle of their marriage.

Types of External Relations

Business Relations: This could be relationships with employers, or own business. Couples form relationships with employers to continue to maintain steady income to operate and run the home.

Faith Relations: These are relationships in the church, small groups in the church and those whom couples serve the Lord together with. Marriages are a mini church, the couple must be a part of a larger body of Christ, whether in small groups or larger groups to continue to fellowship as a body of Christ and strengthen their marriage.

In-law Relations: These are relationships with the former primary family members. Marriage brings growth and multiplication to families. Godly in-laws can bring growth to a family lineage and further God's covenant with a lineage.

Friendship Relations: These are relationships with friends during marriage. Friendships can be formed when earth belong to a group furthering God's missions on earth

Neighbor Relations: These are relationships with other families living close to the couple in the same neighborhood. There are people you will become neighbors within marriage, couples must consider how to manage neighbor relations in marriage.

Relationships with external parties must be well managed in line with the Word of God.

Challenges to Managing External Relations

Many marriages are robbed on the blessings God brings through external relations because of insecurity. Also, many marriages are under attack because of the takeover of external relations. In this section, we discuss 3 of the top challenges faced with external relations by couples in marriage.

Uncleaving: Uncleaving is a condition where a man or woman fails to leave and make other relationships secondary while entering marriage. When uncleaving occurs, a man or a woman fails to re-order the priority of the relationships in their lives.

Before marriage, it was parents, and children. The relationship between the parent and children are primary. The man may be closer to his father or mother, or the wife closer to her mother and father before marriage.

After marriage, the man must leave his father and mother and be joined with his wife as one. Same with the wife, she must leave her parents and become united with her husband. Many couples struggle with this, and this is creates problems in marriage

Infidelity: Infidelity is unfaithfulness in any realm in marriage, whether spiritual, financial, physical, emotion or mental. Because couples unite in different areas in marriage, any realm where unfaithfulness occurs opens up the marriage to external influences.

Types of Infidelity

There are three common types of infidelity and they are addressed below:

1. *Emotional Infidelity*: Couples are unfaithful on the realms of emotion.
2. *Financial Infidelity*: Couples hide money from each other, they conceal financial information from each other and separate finances. They never unite as one on financial matters.
3. *Spiritual Infidelity*: Where couples never united spiritually.

Insecurity: When you are called into purpose, you will need external relations to work and get into purpose. You will also need to work with others to fulfill their purpose. This is the cycle of purpose, fulfilling your purpose when fulfilling the purpose of others. Where there is insecurity, a spouse will hinder their partner from fulfilling their purpose due to insecurity, jealousy and envy, as a result, shutting down the voice of their purpose. Insecure spouses will do anything to prevent their partners from supporting a cause they are insecure about or envious. You must be able to discern this and bring your spouse into the knowledge of God to overcome all forms of insecurity, helping them understand the unwavering protection of the Lord over your marriage.

Marriage & The Ordinance to Become One Flesh

There is an ordinance of God in marriages that the devil is actively defying today. In the earliest days after the creation of man, God gave the ordinance of marriage in Genesis 2:24 *"Therefore a man shall leave his father and mother and be joined to his wife, and they shall become one flesh"*. Concerning all marriages, God decreed that there must be such unification of the man and the woman that they become one flesh. For a man and woman to unite as one in flesh, this simply means their mind, soul and spirit has become one, considering that the body is the container where the soul, mind and spirit resides. From the beginning of marriages, satan has been resisting this oracle of God and he continues to do that today. The enemy is defying this oracle of God by bringing shame and disgrace into marriages.

Prayer Sets for External Relationships

1. Lord Jesus, deliver me from all the curse of uncleaving that afflicts men in the name of Jesus.

2. Lord, shine your light into all types of hidden covenants that is set to prevent my spouse and I from being one flesh

3. Lord Jesus, shine your light to expose any types of infidelity in my foundation that is set to arise and be destroyed in the name of Jesus.

4. Lord Jesus, close all open doors to spiritual infidelity in the name of Jesus.

5. Lord Jesus, close all doors to emotional infidelity that ruins the destiny of men, in the name of Jesus.

6. Lord Jesus, close all doors, to financial infidelity that ruins the destiny of men in marriages in the name of Jesus.

7. As a man, my relations are seasoned with salt, in the name of Jesus.

8. My external relationship shall be baptized with the powers of the Holy Spirit in the name of Jesus.

9. I shall not be a reproach to the name of Jesus.

10. My business relations are committed to the Lord Jesus, I shall not be the man who brings reproach to the name of Jesus.

11. My relations in the house of the Lord shall bring honor to the Lord, in the name of Jesus.

12. My in-law relations shall be baptized of the Lord's spirit, in the name of Jesus.

13. Neighbor relationships are dedicated to the Lord, my life shall not be a conduit of profanity to my marriage in the name of Jesus.

14. Lord Jesus, the spirit of insecurity shall not thrive in the name of Jesus.

15. Lord Jesus, the spirit of mediocrity shall not thrive in my marriage in the name of Jesus.

Journal

Chapter 10

Worship Altars in Marriage

#1 The Marriage Mystery Unveiled: The Altar of Marriage

Marriage is consummated on an altar. Anywhere two people gather to get married, and there is the presence of witnesses, God's altar of marriage is created, and the Lord descends as a witness concerning that marriage. This is why every type of marriage whether held in the church, courts or at a random place is valid in God's presence.

#2 The Marriage Mystery Unveiled: The Altar at the Marriage Bed

The consummation of the marriage at an altar opens the legal atmosphere for couples to proceed into their marriage bed to unite in the body, soul and spirit through deep sexual exploration. This is the most sacred place in marriage.

#3 The Marriage Mystery Unveiled: The Transfer of Authority

Marriage officially brings the bride under the authority and protection of her husband. The husband becomes the major spiritual authority over his wife on earth, and similarly, the wife becomes the highest ranking spiritual authority on earth over her husband.

#4 The Marriage Mystery Unveiled: The Sharing of Blessings and Curses

In marriage, all the blessings available for the man are instantly made available to the man, and all the goodness available to the woman is made available to her husband. If there are any curses present in any of their lives, the curses are equally shared. At the point of marriage, generational books are revisited, all battles left unresolved are shared between spouses. All the blessings available are shared. This is why certain battles rise up against newlyweds.

#5 The Marriage Mystery Unveiled: The Covenant in God's Presence

The manifest to every marriage is in God's presence. When you get married, God is your heavenly witness, and He keeps the covenants securely in His presence.

This is why the solution to every ailing marriage only comes from God's presence.

The Love from His Presence

Love is found, nurtured, preserved and renewed in God's presence. No matter how beautiful and promising love is, it has to be rooted in God's presence to survive. God's presence supplies the fuel and strength to fan the fire of His love upon marriages. Therefore, couples need to spend their lives right there in God's presence, under His banner and care. This counts as worship to the Lord.

The Joy of Your Marriage is In His Presence

While building worship altars, couples will discover the joy of God's presence, that comes only from the place of spending time in God's presence. A joyful marriage is attainable only when couples spend time in God's presence, individually and collectively. This realm is where worship translates into joy for both spouses. Husbands or wives do not manufacture joy or create happiness. Those who go into marriage with that mindset meet with a different reality. Where couples cultivate an atmosphere of God's presence, the Lord works on each of them to place in each of them the recipe for joy that would be needed to generate joy and swerve each other, which translates into a joyful marriage. This is the realm couples live in sync and the oneness of the Lord, where communication occurs in unspoken words, in smiles, in glances and there is the deeper fellowship of God's love in existence. The Lord God delights in an atmosphere of joy in a blissful marriage and does not want His children to be ladened the sorrows of a joyless marriage, since joy and pleasure are at His Right Hand forever. Where couples express joy, God opens and clears away the limitation created by the fall of man in the beginning.

The Essence of Marriage

Every marriage has a soul. The essence of marriage is the soul of a marriage. It is God's desire for the soul of your marriage to maintain its purity and sanctity in God's presence. The soul of a marriage is the barest form of the marriage. God created the soul of the marriage before the couples themselves were formed. This is where He wrote and ordained the days of the marriage before the couples were born into time. The days assigned and planned out for each person also includes the days they live life as married people. The soul is the place where the marriage covenants are kept, and the soul of the marriage is the most expensive, and invisible part of the marriage. Due to its high cost, the soul of a marriage is the most premium portion of a marriage, and this is what the enemy tries to come for when it attacks a marriage.

The Substance of Marriage

Every marriage is unique and has a substance. The substance of a marriage is the unique identity of that marriage, usually displayed in the marriage's specific purpose. The substance of every marriage can only be found on the marriage's worship altar. Setting up a worship altar is inviting God into your home to come live with you, and to carve out the substance for your marriage. Where there is no worship altar in the family, the devil sets up multiple altars for iniquity and unrighteousness in the family and destroys the essence and substances of marriage.

The Marriage Substance: The Design of the Marriage Destinies:

The substance of a marriage is originally created by God.

Psalm 139:16 NKJV

Your eyes saw my substance, being yet unformed. And in Your book they all were written, The days fashioned for me, When as yet there were none of them.

The substance of marriage is created when the marriage is yet to form. The book of Genesis tells us the story of creation of the earth, an account given to Moses. This is your spiritual genesis period, the time when the days of the marriage coming ahead are written by the couple-to-be. Similarly, the genesis of a marriage occurs before the marriage is formed. The destiny of a marriage may be strengthened or altered in the timespan, the months, the weeks or at a minimum, the night before the very day of your wedding/solemnization.

Marital Bible Study

Consider the case study 1:

Beverly and Alan met at a local bible study group. They seemed to love God and study His Word. They got married at the church. After the wedding was over, Alan began to put together plans for the family's Bible Study sessions, and he suggested 8pm. Beverly contested the time because she had TV shows to watch from 8pm to 9pm. Beverly and Alan disagreed over Bible Study time, so Alan focused on following through. Beverly was discipled by the pop culture shows she watched and brought in the wrong values into her marriage. Her expectations and demands for marriage were against the word of God. When she looked for life answers, she found them on TV shows. This led to unruly behavior, and their marriage suffered.

Think about how empty a life built outside the word of God can become.

The Word of God is a guide for life and for marriage. All marriage knowledge must be founded in the word of God, and the grounds of the marriage must be built on the word of God, for the marriage to thrive. Bible reading is one of the ways you can build worship altars together with your spouse-to-be. When you get into the habit of reading the Bible together, you build an altar in God's Word and God speaks to you through His Word.

The Covenant of Prayer in Marriage

The togetherness of a couple in prayer strengthens a marriage. It indicates the presence of the basic elements of love - bond, agreement and unity - these elements, God does not reject. James 5:16 notes, *"Confess your trespasses to one another, and pray for one another, that you may be healed. The effective, fervent prayer of a righteous man avails much"*

The Covenant of Sex in Marriage

The Lord looked at Adam and thought companionship is vital, so He wants couples to have a delightful sexual experience. Devil steals away God's altar from marriages through the perversion of sexual experiences. What is a bride without intimacy with the bridegroom? What is a church without intimacy with Jesus? Emptiness. A sex life under siege is delivered by spending more time in the presence of God. The couple who has spent time with God have beautiful marriages and emotional connections. They enjoy hanging out with their spouses. There's one exception to this: if one spouse spends so much time in God's presence than the other hasn't, there's going to be a mismatch. Sex was created for marriage. Sex is the only place in marriage where couples access the soul of their marriages. Here's why sex is only for the rightful married couples Sex is spiritual and an act of worship between husband and wife to God. One of the risks to eliminate while you prepare for marriage is pre-marital sex.

> If you have had pre-marital sex - stop it immediately, to put an end to the doorway for the enemy to destroy the soul and substance of your marriage.

> If you have had pre-marital sex with someone else - begin a process of deliverance to

disconnect all forms of soul entanglements that may pollute and destroy the soul of your marriage

Sex is one of the most spiritual encounters you will ever have in marriage. God delights in it, He made it for marriage. The marriage bed is an altar, the sanctuary of your marriage, and the primary place of God's presence in your marriage.

As a key takeaway, sex must never be ignored in marriage, because sex is worship to the Lord. Sex is a worship sacrifice on the altar of marriage. Hebrew 13:4 (*Marriage* is honorable among all, and *the bed undefiled*; but fornicators and adulterers God will judge). The marriage bed must be undefiled. The marriage bed being an altar must be maintained with worship to the Lord. Any altar without sacrifice becomes broken down. Sex is a requirement is on the altar of your marriage.

The Covenant of Sabbath in Marriage

Refreshing times and blessings will come upon our marriage when we take rest as commanded by the Lord.

The Sabbath of the marriage is a time of calmness and stillness in your marriage. It is a time of rest, a time when husband turns to wife and wife turns to husband to declare their love for one another. It is a moment of renewal to usher in the peace and freshness of God; it is your marriage's Sabbath. Many couples live life in stress, and build up the debts of hurt based on a stressful life. Establishing a culture of sabbath opens the door to letting go of stress, and releasing the debts of unforgiveness, canceling all forms of past hurts, solemnizing and declaring peace. This is a day that couples say It is a day indeed to say: I am going to fight for us, and I am going to give our marriage to the Lord so He could renew it. This is indeed an emotional time and it is okay for tears to roll on this day. It is a time where all sort of disagreement, war ceases in a marriage and the rest of God is released.

Exodus 20:8-10 NKJV

Remember the Sabbath day by keeping it holy. Six days you shall labor and do all your work, but the seventh day is a Sabbath to the Lord your God. On it you shall not do any work, neither you, nor your son or daughter, nor your male or female servant, nor your animals, nor any foreigner residing in your towns.

Now it is time to proceed, and reflect on the knowledge of God learned from the first chapter through the last and work out an action plan to execute God's plan for a blissful marriage.

Prayer Sets for Worship Altars in Marriage

1. Lord Jesus, set up your worship altars in my marriage, in the name of Jesus.
2. Lord Jesus, the soul of my marriage belongs to you, take it and use it for your glory.
3. The substances of my marriage shall not be stolen in the name of Jesus.
4. Lord Jesus, let the soul of my marriage be precious and preserved in your presence, in the name of Jesus
5. Lord Jesus, deliver my soul from the deposits of darkness.
6. Lord Jesus, deliver my mind from the imaginations of darkness.
7. Lord Jesus, deliver my mind from the images of pollution ingrained into my mind in the name of Jesus.
8. Lord Jesus, sanitize my body, with the blood of Jesus.
9. Lord Jesus, purify my mind, with the blood of Jesus.

10. Father, redeem my soul from the pollution of darkness in the name of Jesus.

11. Father, protect the integrity of your purity over the soul of my marriage.

12. Father, protect the integrity of your power over the substance of my marriage.

13. Give me access to your presence Oh Lord.

14. Grant us the joy that comes from your presence.

15. Make our heart thirst for you Lord.

16. Bless us with the joy of your presence.

Journal

Get the Heaven's Gateway to a Blissful Marriage Book for Her

Heaven's Gateway to A

BLISSFUL MARRIAGE

WORKBOOK

FOR HER

Second
Edition

Ebenezer Gabriels
Abigail Gabriels

Download and Subscribe to Blissful Marriage App

The Blissful Marriage App offers digital tools to convert all the lessons and knowledge you have received through this book into daily practice to transform your marital life.

Subscribe Now
for unlimited access unlimited marriage video library
at
blissfulmarriageuniversity.com/subscriptions

Blissful Marriage Hosts Events – Conferences, Marriage Worship and Prayer Retreats, Marriage Deliverance Programs, and other Marriage Enrichment Program. **Register for an Event at** *www.BlissfulMarriageUniveersity/#/Events*

Blissful Marriage University is always adding new courses to transform your marital life through deep biblical principles, ministry experience found in the knowledge of Jesus.

KEEP GROWING WITH THE BLISSFUL MARRIAGE DIGITAL COURSES

at

www.BlissfulMarriageUniversity.Com

Marriage Readiness

11 Course Modules

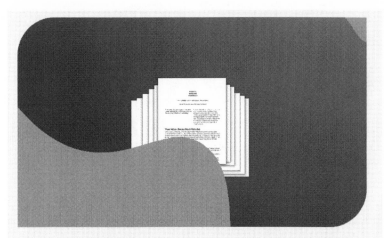

Worksheet: Identifying the Joseph of Your Marital Destiny

1 Course Modules

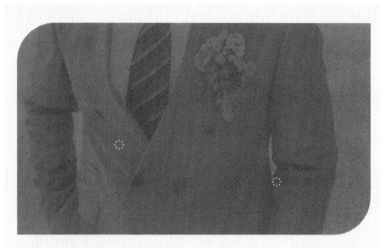

Identifying the Joseph of Your Marital Destiny

3 Course Modules

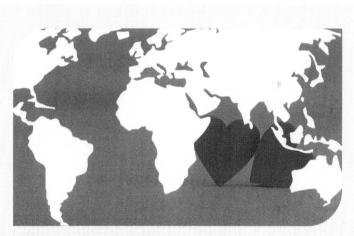

Universal Model of Love

3 Course Modules

Join the Blissful Marriage University Mailing List

https://blissfulmarriageuniversity.com/#/mailing-list

About Ebenezer &

Abigail Gabriels

Ebenezer Gabriels is a Worshiper, Innovation Leader, Prophetic Intercessor, and a Computer Scientist who has brought heaven's solutions into Financial markets, Technology, Government with his computational gifts. Prophet Gabriels is anointed as a Prophetic Leader of nations with the mantle of healing, worship music, national deliverance, foundational deliverance, complex problem-solving and building Yahweh's worship altars.

Abigail Ebenezer-Gabriels is Pastor, Teacher, Worshiper and a Multi-disciplinary leader in Business, Technology, Education and Development. She is blessed with prophetic teaching abilities with the anointing to unveil the mysteries in the Word of God. She is a Multi-specialty Speaker, with a special anointing to explain Heaven's ordinances on earth.

Both Ebenezer Gabriels and Abigail Ebenezer-Gabriels have written over 30 books and some of their works have been translated into Arabic, Chinese and Spanish.

They are founders of the Ebenezer Gabriels Schools of the Holy Spirit and are the Senior Pastors of LightHill Church Gaithersburg, Maryland and Flames of worship Church

They lead several worship communities including the 6-Hour Worship Unto Deliverance, Innovation Lab Worship encounters, Move this Cloud - and prophetic podcast communities including the *Daily Prophetic Insights* and *Prophetic Fire* where God's agenda for each day is announced and the manifold wisdom of God is revealed on earth.

Both Ebenezer Gabriels and his wife, Abigail Ebenezer-Gabriels joyfully serve the Lord through lifestyles of worship and their mandate is to build worship altars to intercede for nations.

Other Books by Ebenezer and Abigail Gabriels

Worship

Worship is Expensive

War of Altars

Business and Purpose

Unprofaned Purpose

Marriage

Heaven's Gate way to a Blissful marriage for Him

Heaven's Gateway to a Blissful marriage for Her

Deliverance from the Yokes of Marital Ignorance

Pulling Down the Strongholds of Evil Participants in Marriage

Prophetic

Activating Your Prophetic Senses

Dreams and Divine Interpretations

Deliverance

Uncursed

Deliverance from the Yoke of Accursed Names

Deliverance from the Curse of Vashti

Deliverance from the Yoke of Incest

Deliverance from the Wrong Family Tree

Principles of Prophetic Deliverance

Mind

Deliverance from the Yokes Deep Mysteries of Creation in the Realms of Thoughts, Imaginations and Words

Spiritual War and Prayers

Rapid Fire

The Big Process called Yoke

Deliverance of the Snares of the Fowler

The only Fire that Extinguishes Witchcraft

No longer Fugitives of the Earth

Subduers of the Earth

Prayers of the Decade

Growth and Advancing in Faith

Deeper Mysteries of the Soul (English, Spanish, Arabic and Chinese)

Men: Called out of the Dunghill

Women: Bearers of Faith

New Beginnings in Christ

Wisdom my Companion

Deeper Mysteries of the Blood

Nations and intercessions

The Scroll and the Seal

America: The Past, the Present and the Next Chapter

Herod: The Church and Nigeria

Prophetic Insights into the Year

21 Weapons of Survival for 2021

2022 Meet the God Who Saves Blesses Shepherds and Carries

About Ebenezer Gabriels

At Ebenezer Gabriels Ministries (EGM), we fulfill the mandate of building worship altars by sharing the story of the most expensive worship ever offered by Jesus Christ, the Son of God and dispersing the aroma of the knowledge of Jesus Christ to the ends of the world.

Ebenezer Gabriels Publishing delivers biblically grounded learning experiences that prepare audiences for launch into their prophetic calling. We create educational contents and deliver in innovative ways through online classrooms, apps, audio, prints to enhance the experience of each audience as they are filled with the aroma of Christ knowledge and thrive in their worship journey.

EGM currently operates out of Gaithersburg in Maryland, USA.

Ebenezer-Gabriels Digital Communities

Explore the Ebenezer Gabriels Platforms

Spiritual War and Deliverance: *www.IAmUncursed.com*

Marriage: *www.Blissfulmarriageuniversity.com*

Children's: *www.inspiremylittleone.com*

Business and Marketplace: *www.unprofanedpurpose.com*

Ebenezer Gabriels Schools of the Holy Spirit and On Demand TV: *www.ebenezergabriels.org*

Made in the USA
Middletown, DE
11 April 2022

63605993R00113